INSTRUMENT OF JUSTICE

By

CB ANSLIE

ISBN: 978-1-962231-03-9 (Hardback Edition)
ISBN: 978-1-962231-04-6 (Paperback Edition)
ISBN: 978-1-962231-05-3 (E-book Edition)

Published by: Crosswords Noble House
Cover Design by: Crosswords Noble House
Interior Design by: Crosswords Noble House

Some characters and events in this book are fictitious and products of the author's imagination. Resemblance to real persons, living or dead, is entirely coincidental and not intended by the author.

Book Ordering Information

Crosswords Noble House
165 Broadway Suite 23rd Floor,
New York, NY 10006, USA

info@crosswordsnoblehouse.com
www.crosswords noblehouse.com
+1 315-537-2705

Printed in the United States of America

Chapter 1

Zach Frederick is my best friend, or at least he was until our last year. We'd been through almost everything together, including girl troubles. So last Wednesday afternoon, when one of the student support counselors called me into her office to inform me of Zach's sudden death, the shock was mind-numbing, to say the least.

Zach had been a country boy—a big strapping guy used to the outdoors, more comfortable with animals than people. The funny thing, his special gift was his hearing. His hearing had the range and acuity of a canine. His primary weakness, however, had always been his heart. Zach had a heart condition. Last Tuesday night, in his sleep, it stopped. *"He didn't suffer,"* the counselor assured me. *"The resident assistant found him about mid-morning."*

This news hits me pretty hard. Feelings of anger and powerlessness still grip me. So, after breakfast, all I can think of doing is walking. My first class isn't until nine; it's 7:30 AM. I head outside, taking the mile-long hiking trail at the far end of the ball fields. The trail wanders through the woods alongside the river. I need to be alone. I don't want anyone to see me cry.

The trail is very familiar; Zach and I hiked here frequently. It's a place we shared where we both experienced the awe of nature and felt at peace with the world. I walk along now in the silent chill of the November air. I kick small stones and dirt out of my way as I go.

A quarter of a mile down the path, I see the dog. He's an Alaskan Husky, big and strong, a beautiful creature. He lives somewhere near the campus. I've seen him before. But today, something's wrong with him. He's stumbling a little. As he turns to face me, there's a wild look in his eyes. That's when I notice he's drooling—white and foamy—from the corners of his mouth.

The hair on the back of my neck rises. I freeze, staring at him, trying to assess the level of danger I'm in. My instincts tell me the husky is rabid. I begin to back up slowly. But he sees me and starts advancing. His powerful jaws open, exposing deadly sharp teeth, as he hurls ferocious growls at me. Fear, then panic, wells up inside. There's not much time to think. Somewhere deep down, something snaps. Instinctively, I reach out with my mind, taking hold of my anger, then refocusing it on the husky... *die!*

The husky is physically strong but can't even comprehend what I'm doing. It's powerless to defend itself against my mind. There is no resistance to my overriding its own natural instincts. I sense how primitive animal thought can be. And I begin to manipulate the dog's demented thinking, sending it charging head-first into a large boulder on the side of the path. Again and again, I force the creature to ram itself into the boulder until it lies dead, less than two arm's lengths from me. I survey its battered skull, smelling the blood that gushes from it. Then I check to be certain no one is around, that there are no witnesses.

Leaving the trail, I'm drained. Yet, the memory of the kill leaves blood on my conscience and will haunt me for years to come.

Chapter 2

Fifteen Years Later

Awaking with a start from yet another nightmare, I give up on sleep. Four hours of rest seems to be about all I'm going to get. Sitting on the edge of the bed, I run a hand through my hair, allowing my eyes to gradually adjust to the darkness.

"Uh..." Mayson moans in her sleep as she shifts in bed beside me. Watching her for a moment, I smile at how awkward her efforts appear. Her swollen belly makes it doubly difficult for her to find a comfortable position. *Nice try, Sweetness.* I lean over and give her curvy hip a gentle pat, putting my hand into the small of her back, expertly rubbing, soothing. *Baby's probably kicking like hell.*

My wife's breathing deepens as she snuggles into the mass of pillows she's managed to pack around herself. I slip a pillow between her knees so it takes some of the pressure off her lower spine and hips. *Well, at least one of us is getting some sleep. Neither of us will be in another month.*

I stand up, stretch, yawn, and tug at the waistband of my gray sweatpants with my thumbs. Crossing the room to the window, raising the shade ever so slightly, I squint into the glowing lampposts that push back the darkness. It's a cold February night with nothing stirring outside except snow. According to last night's weather report, we're supposed to get a foot by the time the storm moves through. *Another hour or two 'til dawn, we may hit that mark.*

My thoughts drift back to the nightmare. It's always the same: *I've just killed the husky when I have a sensation of falling into a dark abyss, and then I startle awake. I remember the feeling of falling in the midst of a menacing darkness, a darkness threatening to obliterate me.* I grimace, I guess it has something to do with what I've done or with who and what I am.

My eyes shift back to Mayson, caressing the curves of her body from across the room. I love her more than I can say. She is closer to me than I have allowed anyone ever to come, but even my wife doesn't know what I really am. I block that from her. I can't risk her knowing, especially when she will be raising our child. *Our child*–that thought terrifies me. *What will he be like? Who will he be like, me or Mayson? Please, dear God, let him be like her.*

Mayson shifts in bed again, obviously uncomfortable. I return to the bed, sit down beside her and place both my hands on her belly, feeling the baby kicking. Sleepily, she blinks her gray-blue eyes open, but they remain unfocused. Her thick dark lashes flutter. Her voice sounds husky.

"Hi."

"You've been restless."

Murmuring, "Baby's kicking."

"I figured. Where can I help most?"

"Small of my back hurts." She rolls over onto her side, facing away from me. "Kid must be sitting on the nerve."

I adjust my position and rub her lower back. Eventually, she drifts off again. *Coffee!* I head downstairs.

Fumbling along the wall to find the switch, I press and turn. Small spotlights in the ceiling fade up. The main level of our townhouse features a kitchen-dining room combination with an island separating them. Four sturdy wooden bar stools line the dining room side of the island. I move around them to the inside. This side of the island accommodates a sink at its center. A butcher block prep area takes up the right end. The rest of the counter space is ceramic. Our coffee maker lives on the ceramic side just above the dishwasher.

After starting the coffee, I grab the remote off the dining room table and click on a flat-screen TV mounted above the patio doors leading out onto the deck. The volume on low. I switch to the Weather Channel: Current Conditions for Friday, February 19...3:48 AM, 28.2° Fahrenheit, accumulation: 8.9 inches... winds: NE at 5 miles per hour.... *Most of our appointments will cancel by nine.* I retrieve my cell phone from the dry sink by the first-floor landing, tap a button, and listen while the speed dial connects with the spa's number. Punching in my administrative code, I change the outgoing message: "Healing Hands Body Spa will open for business at ten o'clock today." I hang up and IM all staff members: Open at ten. Liberal leave is in effect. Mayson will not be in. I'll handle all her clients...Sevan.

Digging the car out takes longer than I expect. By eight thirty the heavy snow measures twelve inches with an underlying coat of ice. The storm lets up as I turn my little Kia into the parking lot of the small office complex where our spa is located, just off Little Patuxent Parkway. The office park's private contractor is already onsite, plowing. There are only two other cars visible, both fully packed in snow. *Glad Mayson won't be coming in today. She doesn't need to be out in this mess.* I shudder at the thought of her slipping and falling on ice.

Once inside the building, I flip on fluorescent lights illuminating a small reception area. The walls, papered with cherry blossom trees in full bloom, are offset by a black carpet. White ceiling panels help give the room an expansive feel. Black blinds covering floor to ceiling windows along the front wall of the building provide privacy. *Got to hand it to Mayson. She's got a knack for decorating...must be her artistic nature.*

Heading behind the reception counter, I replay the messages on the answering machine. Beth, our receptionist, confirms she isn't coming in today. Charlene, one of our physical therapists, will be out too; but Dylan, the new guy, will be in at ten thirty. Dana, our office manager, hopes to be here by eleven. Neither of our two student interns can make it. I decide to let Dylan handle Charlene's clients without my help. I leave him a note to check her schedule.

On the computer, I pull up Mason's schedule: five appointments, three cancellations. My schedule shows six appointments: four cancellations. *Four appointments today, total— barring any further cancellations or no-shows. Bad weather is never good for business.* I turn on the sound system, pop in a whale song cd and set up for clients.

My first client of the day is twenty minutes late, one of Mayson's regulars, Mable Chipton. Mable suffers from fibromyalgia... *so it will be a Bowen.* Bowen, a very gentle massage technique, is ideal for people suffering from chronic musculoskeletal problems. It's the kind of massage therapy Mayson specializes in. Mable, a widow in her seventies with silver gray hair laying in puffy curls atop her head like cotton balls, arrives with a playful grin on her soft rosy cheeks.

"Good morning, Mr. Arkezian. Fine weather this is. Doesn't help your business any, does it?"

"Not really. But it's good you could make it." I smile cheerfully.

"Huh! This is nothing!" She gives a flick of her scrawny wrist. "Charlie and I grew up in Minnesota. Lived there most of our lives. We'd never let a little dusting of snow slow us down. Charlie never would, you know."

"I'm sure he never did."

"How's Mayson feeling? That baby ready to come yet?"

"Just about a month to go; she's not due yet. I convinced her to stay home today. Baby kicked her all night long; her sciatic nerve hurts."

"So, you're going to do me today?"

"Is that ok?"

Mable laughs. "Well, well! Getting a massage from a handsome young man, forty years my junior, with eyes like chocolates and the body of a tennis pro...let me think about this...." She taps the corner of her mouth with an index finger, "...hum, I never remember saying no to chocolate, you know." She arches an eyebrow and winks at me. I have to laugh.

An hour later, seeing Mable out, I hand the paperwork to Dana, who is now covering the front desk. "Please be careful in that parking lot, Mrs. Chipton. It's a bit slick out there."

"Oh, I'll manage You give that wife of yours a hug from me. I'll see her next time."

"I will!" I give a quick wave, walking back toward my office, already punching the speed dial on my cell. It takes a couple of seconds to connect, then rings...*one, two, and three.... Come on Mayson, pick up.*

Mayson's voice grouses at me. "What's with not digging my car out?!"

"I thought you could use the extra sleep. You were having a bad night."

"Sevan, we've been over this. Don't treat me like some sort of invalid."

Calmly, "I'm not. But I don't see the need for you to drag yourself in on a day like this. You know most of our clients are going to cancel or just not show. I figured I could handle anyone who does...."

"Who's been in so far?" The irritation in her voice slacking.

"Mable Chipton. She says she'll see you next time and I'm to give you a hug from her. Consider yourself hugged."

I hear the smile in her voice, "Thanks, who else?"

"Well, all your other clients cancelled, except for Paula Perkins. I expect her sometime this afternoon."

"She's my three o'clock. She always comes on Fridays, at the same time, and she always shows." There is a noticeable pause before Mayson continues, "Sevan, check Paula out carefully, please. It's a Swedish."

Mayson's voice oozes concern. But then, that's normal for an empath -- someone who has the ability to sense and experience the physical feelings and emotions of others.

"Why, what's up with Paula?" I'm instantly curious.

"I meant to tell you about this the other day, but my OB appointment got in the way." Mayson pauses to take a breath, "She came in last week giving off very intense vibes of trauma. And, the week before, it was shock. I've been picking up lots of negative stuff from her: fear, anxiety, helplessness, hurt and pain, but the trauma stuff is new and really strong."

"So, you think something's going on at home." I finish her sentence.

"I think she's being abused. I haven't seen any bruises or anything, so it's not physical. See if you can connect with her, please."

Mayson knows I'm a telepath: I not only read thoughts, but probe memory images as well. I'm a pretty good one too, supposedly a quirk in my genetics, like the empathic quirk in Mayson's. "Alright, I'll try. But we need to talk when I get home."

"Agreed."

Paula Perkins arrives, on time. She steps into the spa in an expensive navy blue ski jacket with matching pants, and a white cashmere scarf around her neck. In one swift motion of a richly gloved hand, she sweeps back the hood of her jacket, revealing short feathered blonde hair with fading highlights.

A pleasant looking woman, Paula wears minimal makeup and appears anxious. Judging from her face, I put her around fortyish. Her grim facial expression makes her look older. The muscles between the eyebrows are pinched, the mouth taut. Puffy skin under her eyes is beginning to darken, suggesting inadequate sleep or possibly crying.

I smile. "Hello! you must be Mrs. Perkins." No response. Instead, she pulls off her gloves and strides up to the counter, stuffing them into the pockets of the jacket. The nails at the ends of long thin fingers are well manicured.

Defensively, "I have an appointment with Mayson."

"I'm sorry. Mayson didn't make it in today. I'm her husband, Sevan. I've been covering all her appointments." I offer my hand, but she ignores it. I let it drop, not pressing the point.

Paula gulps some air. She couldn't look more nonplussed. "I don't know if I should...I usually see Mayson," her voice tremulous. She gives her head a slight tilt. "I feel most comfortable with her." I notice the shudder in the body core.

"Dana will be happy to reschedule your appointment, if you like?" I say, politely, keeping my voice even. "But since you're here, you may as well have the massage. I assure you, I'm a fully qualified therapist. I believe you get the Swedish?"

"Yes. I usually do, but I...."

"I promise I'll do my best."

"Oh! No, no! It isn't you! It's just that Mayson knows ...."

Motioning her toward the hall leading to the treatment rooms, "Come on back." I insist, sensing her resistance collapsing. Reluctantly, she follows.

Our Swedish massage includes hot scented oils applied to the muscles of the chest, shoulders, arms, legs, and back. We use a combination of soothing nature sounds, candle aromas, and natural lighting, from sky lights in the ceiling, to enhance the experience.

The treatment rooms are painted in shades of pink with well-padded tables positioned in the center of the rooms. There are no windows. Music is piped in, scented candles burn in wall sconces. Each room has a bamboo painted floor screen in one corner, for changing. And the doors to each treatment room are black sliding wood panels.

To begin the massage, I first apply warm moist towels to Paula's face and leave them there for a few minutes. When I remove the towels, I apply moisturizer and make pressured movements with my fingertips; I follow this with long concentrated strokes. Cradling her head in my hands, I press firmly with my fingers, completing every press with a drumming motion. I take my time, paying extra attention to the forehead and temple areas. Her muscles feel tense, almost spasmodic. *She's definitely in pain.* I rub gently. Paula closes her eyes and the pinched facial muscles between her eyebrows noticeably relax.

After several minutes, I attempt a mental connection with her: *Paula, trust me.* I concentrate on emanating sympathetic vibes: *I'll understand.* Easing my brain into someone else's, for the first time, feels like diving head first into a giant oncoming wave of static electricity. There's some push back and the jolt will be a combination of my mind's electrical current smashing into theirs: *What's happening? Why are you in such distress?*

13

I stroke her cranium then put my fingers in to the base of her skull where it meets the spine and press. Paula lets out a sudden gasp, and in that instant, like a highly charged burst of electricity, our brain waves sync. I perceive a mental image:

A large, strong man, about 250 pounds, maybe fifty, muscular; he's yelling, Bitch! ...Whore! ... Useless! ... Good for nothing!

Paula suddenly tenses on the table, shoulders arching back slightly. I ease the pressure in my fingers. "I'm sorry. Is that too much?"

"A little; I must be very tense this week. It's been a rough one for me." she says apologetically. *No kidding lady!* I adjust my position, moving my hands away from the nap of her neck, to the muscles at the base where it connects with the shoulders. Every move is calculated and precise.

By the time I begin massaging her back, I have perceived several images of the same man. One image in particular is disturbing:

A man is with a very attractive woman -petite, green eyes, light brown hair, perfectly proportioned—he's laughing. Then, he kisses her. Not just a quick peck on the lips either, he gives her a full blown open mouthed, tongue probing, hand groping, smooch.

Paula's brain waves kick out shock and deep emotional hurt.

Who is he? I coax. I work steadily, using light pressure. Mentally, I nudge: *Is he your husband?*

Paula: *He loves me, really he does. Clay is under financial stress, he drinks and then things get out of hand. Amber's been my friend for years...I've always trusted her. I can't believe he's doing this right in front of me. Oh God! Why would she?*

I interject a reality check: *This is mental and emotional abuse, Paula. Business and economic pressure are no excuse!* I quickly finish the massage and leave the room so she can change. Paula accidentally leaves her cashmere scarf behind the bamboo floor screen.

Later, I phone Mayson. "Clay's cheating on her with Amber, her close friend. They're carrying on right in front of her. Clay Perkins is having financial problems. Paula still thinks he loves her, and it will stop once finances are better. Get this, Paula thinks it's her own fault."

"Classic symptoms of spousal abuse, which means he's done this before," Mayson concludes.

"It's probably been going on for a while," I agree.

"Thanks Sevan, I mean it. It just confirms everything I was picking up from her. Now what do I do?" My wife's voice sounds pleading.

"She has another appointment next week, same time, same day?" I ask.

"Yeah, I think it's one way for her to escape for a while, that bastard!"

"Escape Clay?"

"Yeah," Mayson's anger comes through, like spitting nails. "All her information is in the computer file."

"Gotcha! I'm in. I've connected with her now. It'll be easier to read her, from now on. I planted a reality check in her mind. I'll do her massage again."

"I want you too, but let me do it with you next week, just so she feels safe. Like normal, I mean."

"No!" I say so firmly it surprises even me. "She's got too much emotional baggage going on. It's too intense. I don't want you to take the risk with the baby. I'll take her from here, at least until after you deliver. Look, I need to finish up here; we can talk when I get home. By the way, have you started dinner yet?"

"No, haven't thought about it."

"I'll pick up Chinese. PF Chang's is open. Dana says she noticed it on the way in. Why don't you call in an order? The bistro isn't too far from here; I can swing by on the way home."

"Mayson responds, "I've been craving beef chow mein. Egg rolls too...lots of them!".

It's a few minutes after six when I get home. Making my way from the front door to the dining room, I deposit the bag of Chinese food on the round solid oak table. "Mayson," I call.

"Up here."

I follow the sound of her voice upstairs to the baby's room where Mayson is seated on a step stool, putting the finishing touches on the mural running the full length of the inside wall. Drips of paint and smudges pepper her hands and shirt. I pause in the doorway. *The baby means so much to her, to both of us. This room has become our sanctuary. She's worked very hard on it, and it shows.*

Our baby's room is twelve by fourteen feet with a white stucco ceiling and brand new rust colored wall to wall carpeting. Shell shaped glass sconces in salmon tones, with soft glow bulbs, hang on the walls. The only other lighting comes from the small sky light in the center of the room above the baby's crib. A rocking chair with rust checkered cushions sits in the far corner of the room. The dressing table is positioned in front of the window across from the doorway.

Mayson looks up. I stand beside her surveying her work: a sandy beach covered in starfish and sea shells. Foamy blue turquoise waves, ridden by seahorses on surf boards, roll onto the beach; a boy and girl play in the sand with shovels and pails. The big yellow sun shines from one top corner, and a rainbow beams from the other. Multicolored butterflies, bluebirds and white seagulls sprinkle the open sky.

"Well, what do you think?" she asks.

"Is it done?"

"I think so. I've finished putting in all the planned elements."

"The kid is going to love this!"

"I hope so!" Mayson scans the room, smiling with satisfaction, "It's ready for our baby." She gives a quick shrug of her shoulders and giggles.

Patting her tummy, "It's beautiful," I assure her. "Come on; I'm hungry."

Over dinner we discuss baby names again, for the umpteenth time. Ever since we found out we were having a boy, she's wanted to name the baby after me. Yet, I steadfastly refuse to give our baby any name connected with me, other than my last name. Mayson likes Davit, which translates to David, my middle name.

"...Look, we've already been through this a dozen times. I don't want the kid to have my name. I don't mind if you give it an Armenian name. I'm flattered you want to...but not mine." I can't shake my irrational fears that somehow, if my kid has my name, he might become like me–the me I hide from her.

"Sevan, what's wrong with the name Davit? It is a name that would be perfectly acceptable to both our families, culturally and religiously. What's wrong with that? It's your name for God's sake!" There is insistence in her voice and an agitated glare in her eyes.

"I'm not going to agree to it, period!, I want some more time to think about it." We fall silent. I can't give her a better answer. I don't know myself why I'm so paranoid about this. I just don't want our kid to be like me. I worry that sharing my name will somehow link him to the darker side of me.

We both have Quirky genetics, the combination of which may display in our baby, somehow. Neither of us wants to go there right now. It only took us seven years of marriage to get up the nerve to have a baby.

With a sigh, Mayson changes the subject, "What about Paula? What are you going to do?"

I'm on more solid ground here, "For now, try to convince her that it isn't going to stop if she doesn't take action. She needs to get professional help. I'll keep urging her to every time she comes in, and I won't let up."

"I suppose that's all we can do, but it does seem to be getting worse, and I worry about her."

"I know. It's your nature. You can't help it." I glance over at my wife. Her shoulder-length dark hair is swept back from her face and clipped with a barrette. She wears a deep frown on her ivory face. At five feet, five inches tall with the baby weight carried around her hips, and all the paint drippings she is covered in, from head to toe, she looks comical. I try not to laugh.

"An old wives' tale says a woman carries a girl high and a boy low. Not that I really believe that, I guess. What do you think? Am I carrying high or low?" she asks as she rubs her lower back with her hand.

"Low, definitely low...." *Will he have Mayson's skin or my olive tones? Will he have my eyes or her oval shaped ones? Will his hair be wavy like mine or straight and fine like hers?*

"Sevan, what if he turns out to be like one of us? You know, psychic."

"Then we deal with it. We teach our kid what we know, what we've learned."

"Which one of our abilities do you think he might have?"

"Which would it be worse to have?" I counter. "He could have some combination or maybe none at all. Theoretically, psychic ability comes from a recessive gene."

"Do we send him to IPD?"

The Institute for Psychic Development is where kids, like us, attend school to learn not only academics, but to have the full scope of their natural abilities probed, assessed, and trained. The school was established in the early 1980's with the best of intentions- to nurture and educate psychically gifted children. They only take the good ones; both Mayson and I are good.

The deal is, our education is free in exchange for five to seven years of "service" after graduation. It's all in the contract. IPD has the right to release anyone from their obligation, at any time they choose, for any reason, before the seven years is up. They seldom do, however, with the exception of medical conditions. The most common medical condition is burn out; psychics can suffer extreme burn out. When they show the slightest signs, it's an automatic medical release.

After my mandatory service was up, I chose not to renew my government clearances. They worked my wife pretty hard. Mayson could only handle five years, but that met her minimal obligation. At that point, Mayson was on the verge of burn out. They had to let her go.

Mayson's dark side is that she can get too wrapped up in someone else's feelings and not be able to separate. Once trapped, she could literally go insane. Being an empath magnifies all emotional feelings and physical sensations to an extremely intense level. In women, empathic experiences have produced spontaneous abortions or miscarriages. I don't want her getting too locked in to Paula's situation.

Exhaling slowly, I tell her, "Let's cross that bridge when we come to it." I wipe a tear from Mayson's cheek, kiss her forehead, and wrap my arms around her. *So much to think about....*

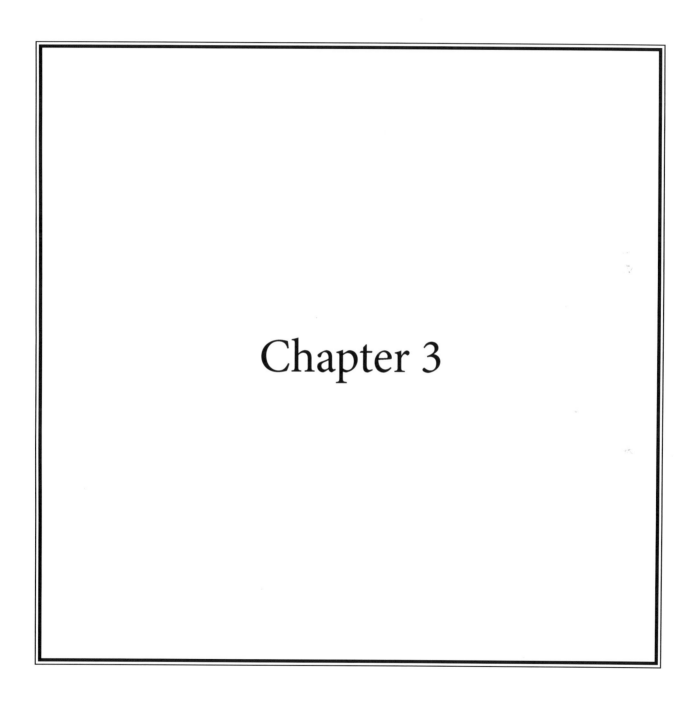

Chapter 3

This morning, Saturday, people are still digging out. The temperature has warmed a bit, up to thirty-eight degrees already, but still cloudy. The sun is supposed to make an appearance later in the afternoon with a high of forty-five.

The streets are passable, with piles of dirty snow lining road sides. Our cul-de-sac, Rumsby Circle, is plowed. I've just finished shoveling out Mayson's brand new minivan and clearing the steps and sidewalk in front of our unit, again. I treated them yesterday morning with a sand and salt mixture to melt ice. I repeat this last step now just to ensure Mayson doesn't slip.

Across from Rumsby Circle is a shopping plaza with a grocery store. I walk over to buy cinnamon rolls for breakfast. It's just about nine o'clock. We don't have to be to the spa until eleven, the normal opening time for Saturdays.

As I reach the bakery counter, I'm greeted by an old man in his early sixties. "What'll it be this morning?" He flashes an electric smile full of perfectly straight, pearly whites. I make my selection and hand him a twenty dollar bill, slipping a note to him along with the cash. The note reads: Sunday confession, four @ Purple Penguin. He counts back change and then hands me a bag with the rolls. I barely see him slide the note beneath the register. "You take care now," he calls after me as I walk away. I smile and wave.

Sunday afternoon, I arrive at the Purple Penguin on route 108, fifteen minutes early. The Purple Penguin is a neighborhood pub. I stand in the doorway searching for an open table.

The tables are dark gray wrought iron with mosaic tops; most seat two to four people. I spy a two-seater in the rear, next to a doorway with a sign lit up in purple tube letters that reads, Restrooms. I make my way toward it.

Slipping into one of the chairs, my back is against the wall.

A waitress wearing jeans and a t-shirt with a purple penguin on the front approaches. "Sam Adams Red," I say. She nods and moves on. A few minutes later, she's back with my beer. I take a few sips and watch the game until he arrives.

I had forgotten how old he must be by now. It has been years since I've seen him. He's in his eighties and wears a gray beard, neatly trimmed, and has short hair. His eyes are dark, like mine. He's short, maybe five feet, five inches tall with a bulbous nose. The Confessor is wrapped in a heavy, dark gray wool coat and has a crimson scarf around his neck. He holds a cane in his right hand, yet his gate is steady, deliberate. When he reaches the table, he takes a few minutes to settle into his seat without removing his coat or scarf. I wait patiently.

The waitress returns; he orders Smirnoff on the rocks. After she delivers his drink, he takes a swallow, letting the liquor roll down his throat, like wine cleansing his palate. "Ah," he gives a satisfied sigh. "Good stuff. Warms my old bones and lubricates achy joints." his eyes shine as he smiles at me. I nod.

"So, you need confession?"

"I need advice and confession."

"Ok, confess first and then I give you advice."

"Thanks for coming by the way. I know I haven't been...."

"No problem." He puts up a hand to stop me.

"I know you and your family. I've known you since you were a baby. I helped marry you."

I take a swig of beer. "My parents consulted you before they signed me up with IPD."

"I remember."

"My last year at IPD, I had a bad experience." I pause. "I learned something about the darker side of my gifts. IPD didn't discover it. Mayson doesn't even know. I've never told anyone about it. But we're expecting our first. It took us a long time to have a baby because we're both afraid of what it might inherit, genetically, I mean. You know Mayson is an empath."

"Yes," his head inclines forward.

"Anyhow, I have this crazy idea that if we name the kid after me, somehow it might inherit this darker aspect of me.   It's silly, stupid, and irrational. I know that, but I just can't shake it."

"Not so silly as you might think; that's been a belief held by many for centuries. People attach the name with personality characteristics, good and bad. That is why children are often given the names of dead relatives."

I take a few moments to let that information sink in. "Well, Mayson and I are arguing over names for the baby. She wants to give the kid an Armenian name, but I won't let her name him after me. She really wants to because Davit is a perfectly acceptable name to both our Armenian and Jewish backgrounds."

"Yes, yes I can certainly understand the dilemma."

"Can you give me a name that will satisfy her?"

"Well, sure. I knew most of your family members. I knew a distant uncle of yours; his name was Hurik. And he was exactly that, a small fire. If you don't care for that one, another family member, on your dad's side, was Mark. If that's all the trouble, you could have just called me up on one of those cellphones people are always using these days."

I take a deep breath, "It's this darker side of me. I can't deal with it. I don't know what I am supposed to do. Why me? It's giving me nightmares."

"Nightmares, you say?" The Confessor looks a bit more curious.

"Is our conversation covered by confessional rites?"

"Absolutely! What you tell me will go to my grave with me, which may not be too long from now." There is a rather prolonged silence between us.

"I've been hiding the truth about myself for so long that at times I can't stand it anymore. I hide it from everyone. And, there is now, this cold dark place within me that I can't ignore. I tell him about the abyss in my dream, "...I don't know why me, why I...."

"You are in serious pain," he observes, the shine fading from his eyes. "I'll see to it that daily prayers are said for you."

"Pray for me to have the wisdom to know what to do. Please, pray hard."

"I give you my word. Do you want absolution for something you have done? Have you committed a sin?"

"Yes, I have sinned. I killed an animal." I whisper.

"Killed?" His eyes probe mine momentarily. Then with understanding, he reaches over, takes my hand in his for a moment, and squeezes. "From this sin, your soul is absolved. Take comfort in that knowledge." He makes a quick sign of the cross over me. "Remember that God gives each of us what we must have to complete his purpose for us." The Confessor let go of my hand, takes the last sip of his Smirnoff, stands up, and leaves. I pay the check.

During Paula's next appointment, she reveals that she has seen a psychiatrist and is on anxiety medication, including sleeping pills. I perceive a newer, even greater trauma:

I came home the other day from the psychiatrist and found them in our bedroom. I found them in our bed! He was having sex with her in our bed! I can't take this anymore. Make it stop!

Make it stop! God! Please make it go away! Paula is shivering, uncontrollably, on the massage table. There seems to be no way to calm her.

I suggest: *Leave him. Go stay with someone, a friend, a relative. But, don't go back there; don't let him do that again. File for divorce. This is emotional and psychological abuse, Paula.*

Getting my message through to her proves unsuccessful. Her thoughts are clouded by medication and underlying destructive impulses are erupting all over the place, like lightning bolts randomly striking. She's mentally and emotionally out of control. I break off the connection. *I'm not getting through. She's unreachable right now.*

Once she leaves, I make a call to the police giving them her name and address; I describe her fragile emotional state and ask them to swing by to check on her later. When police arrive at Paula's home, they find her body in an upstairs bedroom. Paula Perkins is dead from an accidental overdose of sleeping pills. Clay Perkins is not home.

When I receive the call from Howard County police, in the dead of night, while lying in bed, still groggy with sleep, the dark cold space inside me explodes with one singular emotion, rage. I slam the phone down.

"Damn it! Fucking Son of a Bitch!"

"What? What happened?" Mayson is immediately wide awake beside me.

27

I don't mean to break the news to her telepathically, but I can't make the words come out. Having linked our brainwaves so many times in the past, we are so familiar with each other; the connection is now seamless, almost automatic.

Once she knows, Mayson feels sick to her stomach; she jumps out of bed and races to the bathroom where she retches. Following behind, I stand beside her and hold her, keeping her hair out of the line of fire. When she's done, she turns and collapses in my arms, her body crumbling with heavy sobs. I stroke her hair, wiping her mouth with a towel, as we slide down on to the bathroom floor, clinging to each other.

The tears in my eyes are not for Paula. They are for Mayson and me, for our fears of losing our baby, *Think about the baby. Let me hold the pain; send it to me; protect our baby.* I stay inside her head, holding our brainwaves in sync, using every ounce of psychic energy I can muster to soothe and console. I fill our joined thoughts with every happy memory I'm able to invoke, pushing out negative thinking, refusing to give rise to emotions of loss or sadness.

Slowly, ever so slowly, Mayson begins to respond. We commune with memories... *making angels in the snow, chasing each other to rub snowballs into each other's faces, drinking Irish Coffees by a stone fireplace....* And, behind it all, in that part of me I have always kept from her, I contain my rage, her grief, our pain, our fear and despair. I keep it contained; drawing it out and away from her, away from the joyful happiness that I want for us.

Chapter 4

Monday morning, Clay Perkins tries to cancel Paula's next appointment. Beth transfers the call to me.

"I would be happy to cancel the appointment, Mr. Perkins, but it has already been paid for," I lie. "We have a no refunds policy."

"Well, can't you make an exception in this case? You do understand that Paula has passed."

"We are deeply sorry for your loss. Perhaps you would like to keep the appointment yourself; it might prove very beneficial for you right now." *I want to meet you, you bastard! I need to know why you drove your wife to commit suicide! I'm just dying to know!*

"No thanks. I don't want a massage."

"Perhaps you would like to gift that time slot to someone else?"

Clay Perkins is silent for a moment before replying, "Come to think of it, Paula's friend...Amber's taking her death pretty hard. Maybe she can take Paula's place...this Friday you say?"

"Friday at three o'clock; the friend's name?" I prod.

"Amber Fagan," he snaps. "I'll see she's there at three on Friday."

"Alright then, we'll expect her."

Amber? Isn't that the name of the other woman? What a bonus; I may be able to find out why a woman would betray her friend. Why would she do it? It's what Paula wanted to know. And, eventually, maybe I can get him to come in too.

Amber Fagan looks exactly like I glimpsed her in Paula's memory: very well put together, slightly younger than Paula, with expressive eyes that appear troubled.

I do not attempt to connect with her during this initial massage. Instead, I concentrate on relieving her stressed muscles, which takes a considerable amount of work; her back and shoulders feel hard as rocks. I chat pleasantly to calm her and cultivate a professional rapport. Then I do my best to persuade her to come back, to become a regular client.

"Will the same time next week be good for you?"

"Ah, I don't know. I ah...didn't think he'd... I mean, I didn't realize I'd have to come every week."

"You don't have to, but don't you feel much better now?" I flash my most ingratiating smile.

"Yes, yes I do feel better, thanks," she says, her voice smooth; her smile, faint. "I guess it wouldn't hurt to come next week...." She's hooked. I walk her out to the receptionist. "Beth, put Ms. Fagan down for the same time next week." "Certainly," Beth quickly makes the appointment before Amber Fagan can object or change her mind.

On my way back to my office, Dylan hands me a note from Mayson:

Having contractions. On my way to see my OB; she thinks they're just Braxton Hicks. Don't worry; this is part of a normal pregnancy. Call you soon.

I feel a wave of anxiety surge through me. Air escapes my lungs so quickly that my chest hurts and my head starts throbbing.

"How long ago did she leave?"

"Just after you started your last session," Dylan is definite.

"Who's covering her appointments?"

He gives a quick tilt of his bearded chin, "You just did. Remember, her last appointment on Fridays used to be Paula Perkins."

"Right, that's right. Sorry." Shaking my head, "My next appointment would be?"

"Don't know. I can check with Beth."

"Never mind; let Beth know I'm leaving."

"Done."

Mayson fumes, even as she lies on her left side in our bed sipping ice water. The blue and white patchwork quilt, which normally covers our king size brass bed, has been turned down. She is lying atop the blue satin sheets. I enter the room, crossing the navy blue carpet to the bed, as my wife informs me that while the contractions may have been Braxton Hicks, upon examination, her doctor noted the baby has turned and dropped already. "My cervix is showing signs of opening. The baby can come any time," Mayson announces.

"My doctor has ordered me to stop working. I'm now on bed rest."

I feel a weight fall from my shoulders. *Thank you doctor! There's no way my wife can accuse me of being over protective.* And I don't have to fear her getting too wrapped up in clients...my primary concern since this pregnancy began.

Mayson senses my relief. Staring at me, "Don't say it!" she growls as I sit down on the bed beside her.

"Moi?" I feign innocence.

Sticking out her tongue at me, "I already let Beth know. She's clearing my schedule."

I read frustration in her eyes. "Look, it won't be that long. You'll be back to work in no time. That's why we hired Dylan. He'll pick up some of my client load while you're gone. I'll handle the Bowens. We planned it. It's just happening a little sooner than expected."

"What am I going to do for the next four weeks? I can't just lie around. I can't! I'll die of boredom!" I read a trace of panic in her mind: *You need the time to rejuvenate. Paint, you're good at it. You love it, and you know it calms you.*

She's tearful, "How can we have the baby when we don't even know what to call it?"

"Ah, that's what's upsetting you? Well, I've been thinking."

"Oh?"

"I meant to tell you. I have a name for you."

"You do?"

"I had a distant uncle named Hurik. It means little fire. By all accounts he was exactly that. And another relative named Mark. What do you think?"

"Little fire...Hurik...Mark Hurik." She mulls this over for a moment; a little twinkle creeps into her eyes. "I like it. I do. It feels just right." I tickle her ribs. She squeals and squirms away from me, "Yes!" I tease. I grab her glass, set it on the night stand, and then attack her and tickle some more, "You know you love it. Say yes!" Laughing, she eventually gives in, "Ok...Ok...Yes! Yes!"

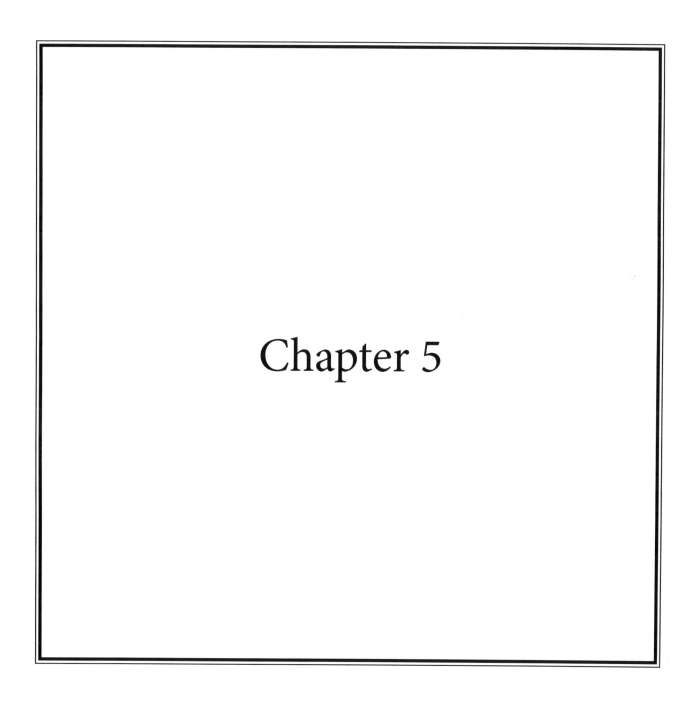

Chapter 5

Amber Fagan's arms have fresh bruises on them. They're blackish blue with tinges of yellow and green. I work the warm massage oil into the soft supple skin of her arms, very gently, avoiding the bruises. Then, I focus my attention on her legs. They're long with a touch of dry skin on the shins. Her calf muscles are very tight, as are the thigh muscles. I work them. There are bigger, nastier looking bruises all over the inside of her thighs.

Finally, I'm ready to start on her back, "Sally, my assistant, will help you turn." Not waiting for a response, I slide the treatment room door open and call, "Sally, your help with Ms. Fagan please!" Sally, an Asian girl of about twenty with a prim look, races half skipping, half running, down the corridor as I move away from the doorway to the treatment room. While I wait in the hallway, Sally helps Amber reposition herself on the table and then leaves.

I begin working on Amber's back, and at this point, make an attempt to mentally connect with her: *There are quite a few bruises on your thighs and arms that weren't here last week.* I stop as I feel the static of her brain waves –strained, overpowering. In someone who is emotionally vulnerable, as she is now, I know that when the timing is just right, a connection can occur with a minimized jolt. *How do I want to approach it? Chopping ought to do it.*

Performing a chopping motion on the mid-back and shoulder areas has the effect I desire; her thought pattern is momentarily interrupted giving my brain waves the opportunity to slip in with hers. I keep up the chopping motion long enough to allow our brain waves to fall into sync: *How did you get the bruises Amber? Did Clay do this to you?*

Amber is hesitant: *…He likes doing it hard.*

He likes doing what hard? I urge.

Clay likes his sex hard and fast. It's painful. He leaves bruises. I've pleaded with him to stop, *but he doesn't care. He did that to Paula too. She told me about him a long time ago.*

Was Paula your friend?

We were friends.

Good friends?

Pretty good friends.... Her facial reaction is disgust, almost horror.

I urge: *What did she tell you about Clay?*

He only thinks of himself. Suddenly, she shuts me out; there are tears running down her cheeks.

"I'm so sorry! I didn't mean to cause pain." I stop the massage and get a tissue from a side tray of the table. Handing it too her, "Is there a particular spot that I touched where it hurts more?"

Lifting her head off the table, taking the tissue, she wipes her cheeks, "No. No. I want to go now."

"Of course, I'll see you next week."

She doesn't respond. *Not good. Will she show up next week?* I wait for her to change, then walk her out to the reception area and stand there while Beth schedules her next session, all the while knowing that just because she has an appointment doesn't mean she'll keep it. *Damn!*

A buddy of mine, Kip, works as a private detective. I put in a call to him: "Do me a favor, run some backgrounds for me."

"What's up pal?" Kip's cool.

"Got a client situation I have funny feelings about," I say.

"Now man, you know you don't just get funny feelings. What gives?"

"Need to understand who I'm dealing with, ok? If anything comes of it, you'll be the guy I call."

"Fair enough...who we checking?"

"Clay Perkins and Amber Fagan..." I feed Kip what contact information I have.

"How long?" I ask.

"Couple of hours, day maybe...email ok?"

"Good enough."

"You'll get the bill too," he laughs.

"Right," I hang up.

Clay Perkins' background is clean. He's an independent security systems consultant who pays his bills on time and enjoys the occasional game of racket ball. There's nothing on him, not even a parking ticket.

Likewise, there's nothing alarming about Amber Fagan's background either. Her one and only five-year marriage ended in divorce, no children. She is the vice principal at a local middle school with a solid personal and professional reputation. Nothing earth shattering.

I digest this information slowly. *Clay's clean public record doesn't bar him from being a brute; he's been lucky, never been caught. Paula was obviously afraid of him and never filed any complaints against him. How then does he keep Amber under his thumb? That's the million dollar question. He'd have to have something on her. What's he got?*

If Amber is telling the truth, and I believe she is, she could be in real physical danger. It had been a long time since he was physical with Paula, but he has recently been physically abusive with Amber. For her own protection, I'm going to have to drag it out of her during her next massage, that's if she shows up.

On Friday, Amber is running late. I start to think she might be a no show when Beth buzzes me. Amber has arrived. It's 3:20 p.m.

"Will you take her?"

"Yeah, push back my four o'clock."

"You got it."

I begin the massage by working the facial muscles. "Ms. Fagan, is there any particular area you want me to pay special attention to? Is there any particular place that hurts?"

"My lower back seems to be a little sore, more so than usual."

"Ok, anywhere else?"

"That's all."

I continue massaging the scalp, face, and upper neck. As I do, I press my thumb into the space where spine and brain stem join: *Tell me about Clay.* I hold the pressure on point, with my thumb, and force mental contact. She shudders on the table. My mind penetrates her thought patterns, and I wait for us to sync:

Tell me about Clay.

Tell?

He hurts you during sex?

Yes.

You were friends with Paula. What happened?

She grimaces. *Clay happened.*

Let me see...show me.

From Amber's memory, I see:

She's having drinks with Clay and Paula at the Purple Penguin. They have a table in the front of the dining room, near the window. Clay is seated between the two women. Paula looks sullen, her eyes half glazed, vacant. She's silent.

Clay smiles. He stares at Amber's hair which is tucked up under a tan newsboy hat. His gaze fixates on Amber's bust. Amber feels self-conscious; she adjusts the green knit shrug she wears overtop a long sleeved tee. They have another round of drinks. Clay places his hand on Amber's knee, under the table. He squeezes.

Soon, Clay calls the waitress over and orders a large deep dish pepperoni pizza. When the pizza arrives, Amber adjusts her chair so as to be out of Clay's reach. He moves closer. Under the table, he places his hand higher up on her thigh. He grabs hold and squeezes again, harder. Amber audibly gasps at the discomfort this squeeze generates. Gruffly, Clay says, "Don't move! I like it this way." He continues to knead her thigh, ignoring clear signals of pain.

As they leave, Amber nervously fumbles with her car keys and accidentally drops them. Clay retrieves them but refuses to return them to her. "Paula, take our car and go home." He hands Paula his keys. "I'm going to take Amber home." He ignores Amber's protests. Paula quietly accepts the keys from Clay. A few moments later, she drives away.

Clay slides into the driver's seat of Amber's car and drives to her house. After parking in the driveway, they walk to the front door. Once inside, he locks the door and grabs her by the throat, throttling her. The hat flies off her head, rolling across the slate floor of the foyer; her hair shakes loose, falling around her shoulders. Amber desperately struggles to free herself. He squeezes and shakes her, "Don't make me hurt you. Promise not to scream and I'll let you breathe, ok?" Amber gives as much of a nod as she is able. He eases his grip, and she gulps in air; suddenly she tries to bite his hand. Angrily, he drags her into the living room, shoves her to the floor and falls down on top of her, pinning her.

One handedly, he removes the belt from his pants. She struggles with him, but somehow he is able to wrap the belt around her throat. Pulling the strap through the buckle, he tightens it. "Stop struggling or I'll make this very quick," he snarls. Amber is still.

He turns her face to his and kisses her, repeatedly. Then he commands, "Take all your clothes off, everything. Do it slowly." He tugs on the belt a little; she gags and begins to rise.

Once she's naked, he tells her, "Lie back down and spread your legs, wide." Amber lies down and spreads her legs. "That's not wide enough! Wider!" he demands. She obeys, spreading her legs as far apart as she possibly can. He drops his pants, and kneels between her legs. Bending over her, "Don't move…I've been planning to take you for a while now and I want to enjoy it." He begins kissing and nuzzling her breasts. Clay rides her hard; thrusting deep, banging her with as much force as he can, for as long as he can. When he finally comes, he collapses on top of her, clinging to her breasts like they are handle bars on his favorite bike. And as a last indignity, he gets off of her and turns her onto her stomach. He uses the belt on her. Amber squirms and cries the whole time.

Clay rapes Amber repeatedly all night long. At the end of each sexual episode, he whips her with the belt, until he has lashed her just shy of bloody, indifferent to where the blows land.

In the morning, he calls Paula to come pick him up. As he leaves he says, "You know I'm tired of Paula; she bores me. Accidents happen to people, and Paula's accident prone. You're her best friend. You don't want accidents to happen, do you?"

"No."

"As long as you are good to me, Paula won't have any accidents, any really bad ones. You wouldn't want that on your conscience now would you?"

When the connection breaks, Amber is sobbing. I whisper to her, "I know what happened. I can help you. Just keep playing this out with him for another week. Can you do that?" She doesn't answer, but she gives a slight incline of her head. "One more session is all I need. I have to know exactly how he did it."

Amber Fagan is both brave and terrified. She has every right to be; I know now that Clay killed Paula, but I need to get the detailed picture. Amber is in real danger. She carried on with Clay, not to hurt Paula, but to try to protect her. As strong as she is, her weakness is that she couldn't, and still can't, live with the idea of Paula having an accident because of her.

And Clay still has a hold on her because he's probably making her feel guilty. He's making her feel she's responsible for Paula's death. *What a monster!*

Chapter 6

I call Mayson to let her know I need space. "I'm going to stay at the spa tonight." Her disappointment is evident even over the phone, but she understands. She knows as well as anyone that sometimes we psychics need to be totally alone. I know she can sense that need in my voice now; I pray it's all she senses.

She huffs, "Call me tomorrow."

"I will. If the..."

"If the contractions start, I'll text you. Don't worry; I'm not having this baby without you. You just take care of yourself."

I buzz Sally and send her to pick up beer and a pizza. "Just put it in the lunch room for me," I say, handing her cash.

"Sure thing," but her face expresses confusion. "Hey, is everything ok with you and Mayson?"

I know she's genuine. She's also not psychic. "Yeah, we're good. I just need to be alone for a while."

"Back in a bit," she takes off.

Pounding something is the only thing on my mind. I'm sickened by what I have gleaned from the minds of both Paula and Amber. My rage is boiling over. Working it out physically is the best way to maintain control. And for Mayson's sake, for the baby, I have to maintain control. So, I visit the physical therapy room, a large open space area with all the latest equipment, including a punching bag. It's the only room in the spa with black walls, like the blackness inside me.

There are no clients in sight. The room is entirely empty. Dylan and Charlene have already left for the day. Dana is the only other person still here, besides me. Crossing over to the punching bag, I imagine it to be Clay and begin hammering away with my bare fists. I go at it as hard as I can, feeling better with every punch, until my knuckles start to bleed. When I finally stop, chest heaving and fists dripping blood, I stroll out to the front where Dana is about to leave. "I'll lock up," I tell her.

At the back of the spa right next to the emergency exit is a half-bath with a shower. It's here also that the stacked washer and dryer live. Both Mayson and I keep a couple of clean changes of clothes on hand for emergencies. So, I peel off my sweaty clothes and toss them into the washer. After a quick shower, I change into a gray sweatshirt and blue athletic pants.

Next door in the lunchroom, which is really a kitchen with a small table and chairs, I scarf pizza, washing it down with beer. The lunchroom has a flat screen TV, still on. With indifference, I watch the news and then surf channels until I find a basketball game. My absent stare at the monitor is disrupted by the end of the game, about nine thirty. Switching off the TV, I cross the hall to the office I share with Mayson.

Our office is painted white. A large rectangular window at the far end of the room has black vinyl blinds, tightly drawn. Under that window sits a black metal framed futon with a leaf patterned covering and two large matching pillows. An afghan lies neatly folded over the top of the futon. Black end tables sit on either side with lamps atop each. Ignoring the work stations on opposing walls, I head straight down the center of the room to the futon and unfold it. It's early for bed, but I'm exhausted. I set my cell in a charger on the end table and sprawl across the futon. Pulling the afghan over me, snuggling into the pillows, I sleep without dreaming.

Chapter 7

Amber Fagan's third visit to the spa is exactly three weeks after Paula Perkins' death. I eagerly await her arrival. It is absolutely clear that Clay Perkins drove his wife to suicide. But how Clay pushed her to do it is the question I hope to have answered today. The key to this question is locked up in Amber's memory.

When she arrives, Amber is noticeably uncomfortable. Before the massage begins, I send Charlene in to assist her and rub her down, from head to toe, with numbing cream. When Charlene exits the treatment room, her facial expression tells me everything I need to know. *Clay has whipped her again, badly*. I decide to confine the massage to the face, neck and shoulders. I also instruct Charlene to make an anonymous report to the police.

Amber's mind is fragile. Establishing a mental connection is not difficult, but wading through the debris of emotions proves challenging. She's frightened to the point of hysteria. With extreme gentleness, I massage her face and neck:

Why did he whip you?

I told him Paula is dead and I can't prevent any accidents.

And that provoked him?

He made me have sex with him, continuously, all weekend; any time he wasn't inside me, he was whipping me. She begins tearing. *Help me. I can't take this anymore. He's going to kill me just like he did....*

Just like he did Paula? She chokes back sobs.

Show me.

It's the Perkin's living room. There's a bay window along the front wall of the house. The window is dressed with heavy brocade curtains and white shears. The drapes are not completely closed.

In front of the window is a round Victorian table made of cherry. On the table rests a tiffany lamp which gives off a hazy glow. On either side of the table are two large wing-back chairs- one covered in rich burgundy fabric with gold cross stitching running throughout. The other is covered in a creamy fabric with green and gold stripes. Along the left wall, there is a red brick fireplace with white trim. In the corner of the room, by the fireplace, sits a beverage cart with four crystal glasses and three decanters full of liquor.

To the left of the fireplace is a green leather couch, at the end of which is a second cherry Victorian table and tiffany lamp. Forming an 'L' shape with the couch and table is a smaller two-seater, also in green leather. An expensive oriental rug lies in the center of the room covering a well waxed wood floor.

Paula sits on the smaller couch, next to the table. Her hair is tied back giving her facial features an austere look, every bit as severe looking as the plain blue A-line dress she wears. She is shaking uncontrollably; her eyes fearfully follow her husband's every move. Clay paces the rug, a bottle of pills clutched in his hand. He's angry. Then a wicked smirk spreads across his face. Amber sits in the winged-back chair nearest the beverage cart; I can sense her feelings of desperation.

"Did you really think I wouldn't find out?"

"I was going to tell you. I just needed something to calm me." Paula pleads.

"Well, if you need something to calm you, why not have a drink?"

"I uh...I needed something a little stronger."

"Amber, fix a drink for Paula, make it a strong one….no ice, no water, straight whiskey." He turns to Paula, "That ought to do." Amber rises out of the chair, slowly, and goes to the beverage cart where she pours a glass of whiskey. Her hands tremble; some of the whiskey spills out, running down the sides of the glass. She wipes the glass with a paper napkin from the cart. Then, she brings the drink to Clay, who puts it in Paula's hands.

"You're quite a problem for Amber and me, Paula. Do you know that?" Paula's face turns ashen.

"She's a good friend." He nods in Amber's direction. She knows how accident prone you are and tries to help prevent any further accidents you might have, while you're off spending my hard earned money on psychiatrists and pills. Don't you feel a little bit guilty about that?"

"I guess so…yes." Paula whimpers.

Clay approaches Paula and begins pouring pills into the glass of whiskey. "Now, I think   you need to do something for Amber to show her how grateful you are for all her efforts…I think you should have a drink."

"Clay, not all that medicine at once," Paula complains weakly.

Clay crosses the room to Amber, stands behind her chair and puts his hands around her throat, squeezing. Amber clasps his hands with hers and gasps for air. "Paula, it's your good friend here. I can't keep both of you. And, I'm bored with you; I prefer Amber. But you decide." As he tightens his grip on Amber's throat, Paula drinks.

"All of it," he demands.

Paula finishes the drink. He lets go of Amber's throat and pours another glass of whiskey for Paula. "Drink up," he laughs. Paula downs an entire bottle of whiskey. When she loses consciousness, he turns to Amber, "You wait for me in the car while I dispose of this baggage."

Clearly, Amber needs protection. She's too frightened to go to the police. She won't press charges because she's mentally and emotionally too broken to take any defensive action. Without her, there's no case. Even with her, there's not enough physical evidence to convict him of anything. I have to hide her for a few days. Clay Perkins will come searching for her. That search will lead him here. *Bring it on buddy! I can't wait to see you, you bastard!* I only have one question left. *Why?* Without hesitation, I call Kip. Together, we sneak Amber out the back door of the building. Then I call Mayson and spend another couple of nights on the futon.

Clay Perkin's attitude is one of extreme annoyance. He arrives at the Healing Hands Body Spa at 9:48, Monday morning. "I want to see Amber Fagan," he booms like an actor speaking to the back of a full house. I can hear him from my office in the back of the spa. Quickly, I make my way to the reception area.

"And you are?" Beth responds politely.

"I'm a friend of hers, Clay Perkins." He bellows.

"Mr. Perkins, I can assure you that Ms. Fagan isn't here."

"Look, the last time anyone saw or heard from her, she was coming here for an appointment. That was Friday."

"Have you tried her home?" Beth does her best to keep cool.

"Of course I've tried her home! Her school called me this morning, looking for her. Seems, no one's seen her since Friday afternoon. Now I want to know what time she left here on Friday!" Perkins wears a gray wool blend suit, blue pinstripe shirt, and paisley tie. He's muscular. Slight touches of gray along his sideburns add to an already commanding appearance.

"Perhaps you should...." Beth starts to buzz my office.

"Mr. Perkins," I interrupt as I step behind the reception desk, "I'm Sevan Arkezian, the therapist who treated Ms. Fagan on Friday. Ms. Fagan left here Friday afternoon, around four o'clock, right after her massage. I do hope she's alright. Have you contacted the police?"

Clay Perkins' face looks confused, "Her school's doing that."

"Is there anything else we can do for you? We'd be glad to help any way we can."

"No, I suppose not." He scratches his head for a moment. "Well, here's my card. Call me if you hear anything."

"We certainly will," I assure him as he stuffs the card into my palm. When he turns to leave, I notice he's favoring his left knee... *I may never get another chance with him.* "Mr. Perkins!" I call after him. "Is your knee bothering you?"

Perkins stops, turning slowly back to me. "It's nothing. Twisted it a little playing racket ball, just sore is all," he grimaces. "It'll be fine in a day or two."

"I can help. If you'd like, I can massage the muscles and take some of the sting out of it. It won't take but a moment. There's a little technique that is just perfect for athletic injuries...." I make my best pitch, guy to guy, "If you're not in a hurry...injuries around the knee joint can be very uncomfortable."

Perkins eyes me for a moment. Finally he gives a slight shrug, "Alright! What the heck! If you wanna try, I'm game."

"Come on back," I signal with the fingers of one hand. He follows me back to treatment room three. Sitting on the table, Perkins rolls up his pant leg. I take a closer look at his knee. It's slightly swollen; the skin surrounding it has turned a deep pinkish color with tinges of yellow on the perimeter. I gently manipulate the muscles while we talk sports. *Get him hooked. Draw him back here again; make a client out of him.* I keep talking, "If you stop in next week, I'll give it another go. It should be good as new after that."

"Right, let's see how it goes."

A week later, Clay Perkins is waiting for me in room two. It's been five weeks since his wife, Paula was found dead in their home. Mayson is due any day now. Once she delivers, I'll have no time to deal with anything beyond sleepless nights and diapers, for several months. I'm on edge. *I have to get inside this guy's head, and I can't wait to do it. Once his knee is better, he won't be back. I can tell; he's just that kind of a guy. It's now or never.*

As I enter the treatment room, I give Clay a nod, "How's the knee?" Clay is on the table in the center of the room with a knee-length terry wrapped around his waist, bare chested. A pillow roll has been placed underneath the injured knee.

"You did a good job. It's much better. Swelling has gone down, and it doesn't hurt as much. I still can't stand on it for too long though. And twisting's a bitch. I figure another treatment can't hurt."

"After this one, you'll need to rest it for a couple of days, but that should be enough to cure you," I assure him as I approach the table and begin the gentle massage. Simultaneously, I attempt to penetrate his brain waves. Breaking into his thoughts is not difficult. What is challenging is redirecting the pattern to the precise memories I need to access. His mind is as murky and erratic as the ocean in a tsunami. Eventually, I find a wave, and I jump into it:

Why did you cheat on Paula? I feel the cold primitive edge of his mental processing and perceive the workings of his Underdeveloped mind.

Who?

Your wife; why did you cheat?

Oh uh, well I needed another woman to...I like to watch um fight.

Fight, why?

You know...just to see...makes sex better.

Then why did you kill her?

Who?

Paula.

I, well you know, um she...I gave her a choice. I gave her the chance to watch Amber die, but she chose to die. She was weak; now, I have to take out Amber too.... He climbs down from the table.

My mind is in shock; I feel the numbness spreading all over, even as I withdraw from his thoughts. I realize Clay Perkins isn't even aware I've read him. His only interest in finding Amber is to kill her. It is the response of a psychopath: a very base animalistic mind, masked by a human body. *If there is a soul there, it is extremely primitive. Clay Perkins is functioning only on the most base level, driven purely by survival instincts.*

Chapter 8

The Confessor and I sip Smirnoff at the bar. The Purple Penguin isn't crowded tonight. There's a small party in the back of the room cheerfully enjoying beer and pizza. I turn my attention back to the old man beside me. The Confessor's face looks more tired than usual; I notice the deepening creases under his eyes and on his forehead. He wears the same gray wool coat, crimson scarf, and carries the very same cane. My eyes come to rest on the cane. For the first time, I notice its long wooden shaft is topped by a gold handle carved in the shape of an eagle's head. *Hum...I never noticed that until now.*

"Your request came through unusual channels. You're lucky I could accommodate. I'm old, but I keep busy," he scolds.

"Sorry, I had a shock today. I need to talk."

"So talk already," he takes another sip of liquor. His breathing is deep and a little raspy. The lingering scent of pipe smoke clings to him. *How did I miss the tobacco...for years?*

I tell him. "I've never known what I was meant to do in life. What my purpose is, it is like I know what I am but not who I am or why. I've always had sensations of disconnectedness: feeling alone. After I killed that animal, I started having sensations of falling into darkness."

"Believers may have fallen, but are never alone," he responds. "Do you truly believe in your heart of hearts?"

"I have so many doubts," I croak.

"We all have a purpose, as time and circumstance may reveal. We are guaranteed a life with purpose; yet the exact meaning may always elude us."

"I don't follow?"

"Just because we are guaranteed purpose in our lives doesn't mean it will be made clear to us what that is, prior to our experiences. The presence of the Light doesn't dispel all darkness from our awareness. In fact, it heightens our awareness of the edges of darkness— where the darkness begins. What the Light promises is to acknowledge us and keep us securely within its array, wherever we are."

"I guess I don't quite get it."

"It is an error of human logic and the arrogance of man to think one should be worthy of such knowledge."

"So, I'm supposed to wander around aimlessly, never having a sense of self-worth," I counter.

"Worth is a value placed upon us by our own minds based on a given social structure. As for wandering, only those without the Light wander."

"Well, I pray for that Light now!"

"Be careful what you pray for my son. Now, out with it! What has shaken you so?"

"Doesn't our faith teach that everyone has a soul?"

He sets his glass down, turns and looks me in the eye, "And...?"

"I'm no longer so sure," I exhale.

"Explain," he encourages.

"I read an animal's mind today, masked by a human body."

He downs the last swig of Smirnoff. He murmurs, "It is difficult to be the instrument of justice. Yes indeed. And so, the time has come."

The old priest reaches into his coat pocket and pulls out a very small vial of liquid. Quickly, he opens the vial, places his forefinger over the opening and turns it upside down. "Close your eyes and imagine light. Concentrate on light, brilliant light. The brightest light you can imagine." With the oil on his finger, he touches my forehead, each eyelid, and my lips as he softly sings:

"Lord now lettest thou thy servant depart in peace, according to thy word: for mine eyes have seen the salvation, which thou hast prepared in the presence of all peoples; a light for revelation to the gentiles, and for glory to thy people Israel" (Luke 2:29-32).

Sevan Davit Arkezian, you are walking in grave darkness; may you one day also walk in the Light. He seals the little vial again and puts it away. He continues, "You do not walk alone. We seldom do. The Light penetrates our darkness, in its own time, usually in some unexpected moment. Let this be of comfort to you."

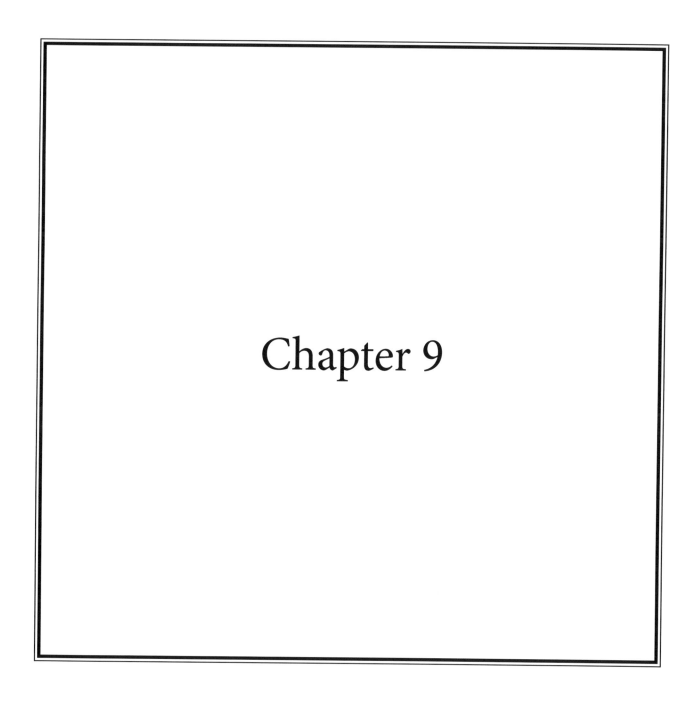

Chapter 9

As I leave the bar, Kip's daily update arrives via text message: Client good. X home alone. I text back: Thanks. Check in tomorrow. Then, I phone Mayson.

"Hello, how are you feeling?"

"I feel like a beached whale, and I look like one too."

"You're beautiful when you're pregnant. Have you eaten anything? Do you want me to pick up something on my way home?"

"No thanks. I'm not very hungry. I ate a bowl of cereal an hour ago. Just come home, please." She sighs. "I miss you."

"I miss you too. Did you get some reading done?" I ask.

"Well, not really. I had this incredible spurt of energy today. I cleaned the entire house."

"You did what!" I don't even try to hide my frustration.

"I just couldn't sit still. I had to do something," she makes excuses.

"Where is the nurse's aide I hired to stay with you today? Why would she even let you out of bed?"

"I sent her home early and cleaned house after she left."

"Mayson! Damn it! You've been home alone all day! I specifically hired her so you wouldn't be alone right now! Don't do that! For God's Sake!"

"Don't yell at me!" Suddenly she is in tears. "I didn't see the need to have her hanging around, waiting on me hand and foot, when I'm perfectly able to do for myself."

"No you're not!"

"I've been on bed rest for three and a half weeks and I can't stand it anymore! Uh oh"

"What?"

"I think my water just broke."

"I'll be there in five minutes."

The labor room is ultra-modern with dim lighting, bright colors and pretty wallpaper; a solid banner of fruits, flowers, and foliage runs across the tops of the walls. Mayson reclines on a tilted birthing table, positioned to help her labor progress. Monitors are attached to her so that her heart beat and breathing are piped through speakers at low volume. A string of nurses scurry in and out, whispering quietly while checking the patient, encouraging us both with happy smiles and pleasantries. I settle into a chair next to Mayson's bed.

A half hour later, I'm at Mayson's side, breathing and counting, the way we learned to in the birthing classes. It is a text book delivery; total time in labor is just about three hours. Mayson does great. The baby weighs in at seven pounds, nine ounces and is eighteen and a quarter inches long. We're both exhausted.

As Mayson and the baby are transferred to a room in the maternity ward, I follow behind, putting in a call to the spa and leaving the announcement on the machine. I spend the night on a couch in Mayson's room with Mark Hurik in a bassinet by her bed. Our little family sleeps soundly.

I awake early, before Mayson. I gently kiss her forehead and take a quick peek at our baby before I slip out. "Tell her I'll be back by three," I say to the nurse as I leave the floor. I have just remembered something important- *Paula left her scarf at the spa, the first time she came, and I forgot to give it to Clay. A cashmere scarf is expensive; I'll bet he'll want it back. Now is just the right time to get it too him. I saw it the other day; it's in the lost & found basket in Dana's office.*

Chapter 10

The spa is empty when I arrive; it's seven thirty in the morning. Using my master key to let myself into Dana's office, I retrieve the scarf. Back in my office, I retrieve the business card Clay gave me with his home address on it. Closing up the spa, I head back to my car and drop the scarf on the front passenger's seat. Cranking my little Kia's engine, I head for Clay Perkins' house.

It's a breezy morning, but the sun is shining, and there are large fluffy white clouds floating across the sky overhead. I stand on Clay's front porch ringing the doorbell, the cashmere scarf in my left hand.

The solid oak door is a knuckle breaker. *No knocking on this door, it's like the entrance to a fortress; any raps my knuckles make will never be heard anyhow.* It takes a while, but finally, the sound of the lock turning is audible. *I think I have to be close enough to see him for this to work. I think so anyway.* Another second and the door swings open.

Clay Perkins stands in the doorway, sleepy and wrapped in a green robe complete with slippers, his hair disheveled. Thick stubbly growth covers his face. He looks a little bewildered at seeing me on his doorstep. Another moment and his facial expression turns to annoyance.

"Sorry to disturb you this early in the morning Mr. Perkins, but I wanted to return something to you. It belonged to your wife; she left it at the spa the last time she was there." I hold out the scarf as I speak.

Forcing myself to concentrate; my eyes scan his body, up and down. I push my way into his thought pattern. His mind is murky and sluggish. It's there, I can feel it. I sense the physical weak point behind his knee, the posterior tibial artery. I envision it puncturing, blood bursting through, flowing from it, unstoppable.

Clay grabs the scarf from my hand, "Christ, it couldn't have waited another hour?"

"Sorry, I was heading to work. I go by this way; figured I'd just drop it off on my way." *Prick! Flow baby flow!*

"Yeah, ok. Whatever...." He slams the door shut in my face.

Flow, come on. Damn it, flow! I force all of my psychic energy into him, even as I get back into my car and sit in the drive. I'm still connecting. Another thirty seconds...*Come on, come on!* Suddenly, I sense the artery give way. Not just a small puncture, but a sizeable split. I feel his blood flowing. I don't let go. I read the panic rising in his brain waves....he knows something's very wrong. Panic grips him; rising to a crescendo...minutes later, Clay Perkins' mind vanishes.

 My head is foggy.... I wait until my breathing normalizes. My head begins to clear, but it aches. I back out of the driveway and head for home. *Paula, justice has been done; justice for you and Amber.*

Setting the alarm, I collapse into bed. As I close my eyes, I begin to dream:

The instrument panel in front of me is lit up. Everything looks normal, the copter engine whirrs loudly. The pilot beside me is smiling. Hey, Sig, I yell. Yeah, the pilot hollers back. What the hell's that? I hear the pilot's scream, Oh Shit! At impact, everything goes black. I'm falling into the darkness of the abyss; it consumes me.

Chapter 11

Traverse City, MI 2004

SIG

I'm a chopper pilot. It's what I've always wanted to be. I can't imagine being anything else. I've known I wanted to fly since I was eleven years old. I knew I'd have to join one of the services to do it, and the Coast Guard just happened to provide the right blend of excitement and challenges. So after high school, it was off to the academy for me.

I've worked hard to make my dream come true, and I'm proud of my accomplishments. Not boastful, I just know I'm good at what I do. Every measure ever set for me, I've met through hard work and determination. I graduated top of my class at the academy, and flying comes so naturally. When I'm in the copter, I have an instinctive feel for it. It's like I meld with the machine or something. I know what it can do, and well, I just make it do it.

My buddies, the guys I fly with, we're a team. We're family. Some of the guys are starting to marry; well, at least starting families. I'd really like to have a family someday. I've had a few disastrous relationships, but that was a long time ago. At twenty-eight, maybe I should be doing some more serious shopping. Mom tells me that the right one will come along, *"When she does, you'll know it."* She's right, of course. I'm not really in any hurry, just lonely now and then. So, I flirt, date a little, but there's nothing serious.

Like I said, some of the guys are starting families, including Dave Mark, my co-pilot. This morning, we're heading over to a local birthing center to pick up his significant other, Kylee, and their new baby girl. Kylee's thinking of naming the baby Rose, after Mark's mom and Tracy, after her own. Mark's not too sure about the names yet. He's still trying to convince Kylee to marry him. For her part, Kylee keeps turning him down. She says, "Having a baby is no reason to get married." She doesn't think Mark's serious enough about their relationship. She knows he loves her, but according to Kylee, "It takes maturity for a marriage to work." *She's right. Mark's not exactly mature. He's just not up to being a dad and a husband. I gotta hand it to Kylee, she's right. I'm glad at least one of them has their head on straight.*

I'm telling Mark my newest dirty joke as we stroll down the corridor of the birthing center. We're still snickering when we approach the sleek counter at the all but deserted nurses' station. One nurse, at the far end of the counter, stares at a computer screen; she has her back to us. Her hair's put up in a surgical cap. I lean my back against the counter as Mark inquires about Kylee and the baby. I hear the nurse get up and make her way down the counter towards us; her soft alto voice responds with words that float through the air like a melody. I roll my body around to face the music. She's a beauty, even in scrubs with a flimsy mask dangling from her neck. My voice fails me, but I still manage to flash a grin and wink at her.

Chapter 12
SKY

He catches my attention right away with his deep rumbling laughter reverberating through the corridor. The uniform clad Coast Guard officer easily jokes with his equally attractive companion. I coyly watch his six-foot-four inch frame lean against the counter. He winks at me. It's nearly the end of my shift, 6:22 AM on a Tuesday in early September. I work as a nurse midwife in a local birthing center not far from the base.

I finish getting the release forms in order, and then I follow them into the patient's room to give some final instructions to the new mother. "...If you would please sign here... and here...remember that you need to call your pediatrician to make an appointment for the baby's first checkup.... If you have any questions or concerns, call this number." I point to the number printed on the form. "A nurse is available twenty-four hours a day...."

While I talk with my patient; the new father cuddles his baby, sitting in a chair by the mother's bed. His companion wanders around the room, smiling at me. He crosses behind me, so close I can feel the stirring of air on my back. My voice quivers a little. The Coast Guard officer steps away and positions himself outside the room, waiting in the hallway just beyond the door. When I leave, he stops me.

"Hi, I'm Sig Baxter," smiling brightly.

"Skylar Arrowson, is there something you need, Mr. Baxter?"

"No. It's Sig. Just call me Sig.

"Sig," I repeat. "Is there something I can do for you?"

"Have a drink with me."

73

This catches me off guard. I take a quick breath, "That's got to be the smoothest pickup I've ever heard."

"I'd really like to have a drink with you tonight." To my surprise, he blushes. "I just think it would be fun, if you're not busy or...."

"Married?" I'm flippant.

"I'm sorry. I didn't think...there's no ring on your finger, so I assumed...."

"It's ok! I'm not married. I just figured that if you're asking me out already, I'd better protect myself."

He stares bashfully at the floor. "I guess I'm being a little presumptuous. Sorry."

"Apology accepted. And yes, I'll meet you at Flames on Torch Lake tonight, say eight o'clock?"

"Eight's good. Tonight then," he gives me a thumbs up and rejoins his friends. *Why did I just accept an offer for drinks with a complete stranger? It must be the uniform.*

The drive to Torch Lake takes longer than expected. Flames, a local pub, is crowded. Tuesday is ladies night. I arrive at half past eight. Ella, the hostess on duty, points Sig out to me. He's alone, sitting at a table in the back corner of the dining room. I smile at him, wave, and make my way over.

Along the way, I pass people seated at heavy wooden tables with smooth rounded tops mounted on rough barrel pedestal, lit by small cast iron lanterns. My boot heals tap as I glide across glowing floors of polished wood. Large porthole windows line the curved outside walls. The center of the dining room features a huge circular stone fire pit where flames dance, playfully.

Sig sips Guinness. Decked out in faded jeans, scuffed brown cowboy boots, and a tee with a bomber jacket, he looks awesome. A man on his best behavior, he's actually standing up for me. "Hi, sorry I'm late, traffic." I smile and slip into a mate's chair across from him.

He grins as he eases himself back into his seat. "No apology necessary."

Our waitress, Robin, arrives. "Hey Sky! So, you're the one who's been keeping him waiting." She winks at Sig.

"Hi, Robin, how's it going?"

"Pretty good...yourself?"

"Fine thanks. I guess you've met Sig Baxter." I smile.

"Well, not formally, 'till now. Thanks for introducing us." She turns her attention to Sig, who beams at her. "Would you like another?"

"Believe so, thanks." He holds out his now empty bottle.

"You want your usual?" Robin directs her question to me, without taking her eyes off Sig. Before I can respond, she heads off to fetch our drinks. There's an awkward moment between us.

"Sky?"

"Most people call me Sky."

"You come here a lot?"

"Well, everybody around here does. There aren't many pubs on this lake." Pausing, "You obviously aren't from around here, are you?"

"No."

I press myself into the curved back of my chair, getting comfortable, as I study him. He has lean shoulders narrowing into a trim waist. His limbs are long and well-toned. His face is handsome, not boyish. His hair is thick and curly, rusty. The high forehead gives way to an angular face with a square jaw. The dimple on his chin softens his features. His nose is straight; his mouth thinly drawn with a hint of mirth tugging at the corners. He stares back at me through mischievous eyes that sparkle like sapphires. I notice how he moves... with precision and confidence.

He's a lion. This thought stirs me in a very primal way. I feel a little light headed, and my pulse begins to race. Butterflies flutter in my stomach. I have a sudden urge to catch my breath; gripping the seat of my chair, I inhale deeply. He's sizing me up too...*I wonder what he thinks?*

Robin returns with two beers. Drinks roll right on into dinner. Before I leave, I agree to see him again.

Chapter 13
SIG

Sunday, I meet Sky at Flames again, around seven o'clock. When I asked on Tuesday, she'd hesitated to give me her number, let alone her address. She didn't want me to pick her up. *She's smart and cautious. I understand. Nowadays women need to be careful. Old fashioned common sense–it's what I'd do in her shoes.*

Sky sits across the table from me now, with a smile on her dewy lips, wearing a navy sweater outlining a full bust. Her skin has a rosy glow. Luxurious dark hair hangs loosely down her back, some strands spraying about her shoulders. Hazel, almond shaped eyes glisten in the softness of the table lantern. She's about five foot four, and I'd guess maybe 125 pounds. The high cheek bones of her face are complemented by a roundness of the chin and jaw. Her nose is short, small-like a slightly blunted candy kiss. ...*So very cute.*

I order a Guinness. She asks for merlot. I start to speak, but she puts a finger to her lips and gently shushes me. We're quiet 'til our drinks arrive. I wait for her to initiate the conversation, uneasy about what the shushing means.

After a sip of wine, "I don't mean to be rude," Sky says. "You see, the custom of my people, when meeting someone, is to observe a moment of silence until our spirits are calm, our minds are clear, and our attention is completely focused on the person we are with. It's a sign of respect. I hope I haven't offended you."

I hear that musical quality in her voice again, a subtle lilt. I nod my head. "How long is this quiet time supposed to last?"

She smiles at me. "Long enough for our drinks to be served."

I snicker. "Ok, I'll remember that." Her laugh is easy. "So, you're Native American?"

"...Not exactly."

"What does that mean?"

"I belong to a people with a very pure ancient blood line. And you?"

"Good old American mutt. Scots, Irish, German, with a little English mixed in there somewhere."

Our waitress stops at our table to take our order; steak with fries for both of us. After she leaves, "So, what ancient bloodline is this?"

"Actually, I'm Eri; Eri is a matriarchal bloodline."

I get a sense there's more to this blood affiliation than meets the eye. But I decide it's too early, so I let it go. "Uh, any siblings?"

"Two older brothers, you?"

"I've got a little sister, just finishing college."

For the rest of the evening, we tell jokes and discuss music, sports, and computer games. Turns out Sky's into baseball; she's a diehard Tigers fan. That's cool, since I'm into the Orioles. So, we compare our teams and debate their chances for the World Series. When we're ready to leave, I walk her to her car. I explain that I'll be busy this week and won't be able to see her until next Sunday. This time, she gives me her number. I promise to call.

Leaning over to kiss her cheek, I detect a trace of sandalwood lingering in her hair. I watch her drive off in her jeep. Then, I hop on my bike, give it a kick, and head home.

Chapter 14
SKY

I come home and take a cold shower. *He's gotten to me way too soon. This was only our second date. But I want to see him again, and a week seems like a long time. What if he never calls? At least I've kept my dignity intact. I won't be just another conquest in this uniformed lion's play book! My new schedule at work will make Sundays the beginning of my weekend. So, there's no problem seeing him next week. I just have to wait 'til he calls, if he calls.*

After changing my clothes, I head for the kitchen and make tea, and then settle down at my computer. It takes effort to push him out of my thoughts. *How can one guy get into my head so fast? I'm not usually this way, not with anyone I've ever dated. But I felt a strong connection from the moment I met him. We'd made eye contact and then, it was as if some current started to flow between us. It wasn't quite electric, but close. Tonight, I had to tear myself from the table and force myself into the jeep. I can't really tell if he felt the same way. I'd like to think he did. What if he didn't? What if it's just me? Don't fall for him alone girl! Just don't!*

Chapter 15
SIG

I think about her off and on, all week. It's hard to say exactly what about the woman impresses me so. It's not just that she's beautiful and smart; although that doesn't hurt. Maybe it has something to do with this old fashioned quality about her, and her voice.... Or is it her curves and those eyes? I can't pin it down. Whatever it is, I'm looking forward to seeing her again.

Mark and I are training, which makes our schedules tight. Also, I know he's so busy thinking about his new baby that he hasn't even noticed my being distracted by thoughts of Sky. *Just as well. I don't need advice, which he would dish out, if he had a clue. I also don't want the news spread around that I'm seeing someone. Spare me the teasing. I'll keep my mouth shut! Concentrate on work; training comes first.*

On our last date, Sky told me she works nights, so I'll wait until around 18:30 Friday to call and ask her to a movie. When I pick her up, I'll stay quiet until we arrive at the movie theater.

When we get to the theater on Friday, as I turn off the bike's engine and we pull off our helmets, I ask if there has been enough quiet time. She laughs at me, rolling her eyes. "Yeah!"

Afterwards, back at her place, we sip Sam Adams and talk some more. *She's easy to talk to, like she understands me. Not sure why. And there's this energy between us. I can feel it. Can she?*

During a lull in the conversation, Sky takes an empty bottle from my hand, strolls to the kitchen and brings me another beer. As she hands it to me, our hands touch. I don't let go right away. She sits down beside me. I put the bottle down on the coffee table in front of me, turn to her, and pull her in for a kiss. Something inside of me is aroused, and I don't mean just sexually. It's primal or something. *Oh Man! I never knew how powerful a kiss could be.* It takes real effort for me to let her go. *I want her so badly I could devour her right here and now. But it would be wrong.* Shame's not a comfortable feeling. *No, I won't cheapen her or me.*

CB ANSLIE

I'll control myself. I want to be sure she wants me too. Anyway, I sense she's holding back a little. If I give her more time, she might trust me enough to let me in.

No rushing this relationship, even if everybody has begun to notice a change in my behavior. I'm a bit of a flirt. Lately, I haven't felt like flirting with coworkers. They're part of the team too, like family, so I'm never serious with any of them. But they all know me. This morning, Becket, whom I tease a lot says, "What's up with you? You haven't even mentioned my bra size this week. Are you sick?" I laugh it off. *I haven't; they're already suspicious. Man! I need to come up with something to say....*

Chapter 16
Traverse City, MI 2004
SKY

It's the end of October. I can now say Sig and I are officially dating. We've been seeing each other once a week, usually on Sundays, because it fits with both our schedules. Yesterday, he called to ask me if he could see me tonight; he's coming to my place, and he's bringing dinner. I told him, "No pizza, Chinese, burgers, fried chicken, or other fast food." He agreed. I'm anxious to see what he comes up with.

At this point, we're comfortable with each other, except for those things about me which I've been hesitant to share. If I tell him, it could be the end of the relationship. Outsiders usually don't react well to this sort of thing. *I don't want to lose him. It'd break my heart.* Yet, it's wrong to keep him in the dark like this. Mom and Faye, my mom's identical twin sister, both agree that even though Sig's an outsider, if I want our relationship to move forward, I need to be honest and straight up with him. There's no choice but to open up. *It's now or never, I guess.* That thought doesn't make me feel any better. In fact, it makes my head hurt.

When Sig arrives at my place, he's carrying a picnic basket, which he sets on the kitchen counter. Without saying anything, he makes a big show of pulling the items out of the basket, one at a time: two bottles of wine, one red and one white; pear slices, a wedge of brie with crackers, quiche from Kroger's bakery, and finally, two gourmet chocolate cupcakes with cream cheese frosting. I kiss him. It feels so good that I kiss him again.

I pull two wine glasses from the cupboard and set them on the counter. Sig opens the wine and pours. We carry our glasses and the food into the living room, making ourselves comfortable on the sofa. Silence fills the room. Finally, I ask him why he wanted to see me tonight.

"I enjoy being with you."

"Is there something in particular you want to do or talk about?"

"I just needed for us to be together tonight."

"Sig, there are some things I think I need to share with you...."

"Does this have anything to do with your being Eri?"

I feel my cheeks burn. "Why do you ask?"

"I had a gut feeling that maybe there was something there when you said it. So I tried looking up Eri on the internet, but I couldn't find anything. I meant to ask you about it."

"Umm, in a way this does. Being Eri is not a tribal affiliation; it's a bloodline. It's the oldest, purest bloodline of healers. There are Eri women scattered among many nations, all over the world. My mom is a healer; her identical twin sister is also a healer, as was their mother before them. I'm a healer too. I've trained for it since I was six. The training starts with learning about herbs and plants and how to use them to heal sick people. Among my people, this is a great honor, something that brings special power and respect. My whole existence is about helping, healing, and nurturing people.

He looks away before he says, "I think I get it, but why's this important? What am I missing?"

He's smart, gotta give him that. I sigh, "It's the power that I have as a healer that makes this so important, so difficult to explain to outsiders, like you." I pause for a few moments, watching his face as he grapples with that idea.

He frowns. "Ok, I'm listening."

"Sig, Eri women have special powers. Some of us are psychics. For me in particular, I'm a clairvoyant. So are my mother and my mother's sister. We all share various degrees of this gift, which we call the sight. We have visions."

I'm not quite sure how Sig's processing these facts. He isn't giving me the usual 'oh come on now' look that most people give those who claim psychic abilities. But I can't tell if he truly believes me either. To his credit, he isn't immediately bolting for the door. I count this as a positive sign.

I change the subject. "The birthing center is remodeling next week. They'll be doing one room at a time. We'll have only five out of six available. Babies don't wait. When they're ready to come, they come...." I try to keep things light. He's quiet while I talk.

We finish dessert around ten, and he heads home shortly after. Once he leaves, I can't help myself, I cry as I tidy up. The possibility of not seeing him again feels overwhelming.

Chapter 17
SIG

Sky's revelation that she's a healer is something I think I'm okay with. She fits the roll, and I'm willing to accept it. Lots of folks are into herbal medicines these days; sometimes that stuff works. I can handle that much, but the visions and psychic part threw me. I couldn't think of what to say. It's not that I don't believe her, but in my world, psychics are crackpots and visions are biblical. Either one makes a person weird or crazy. Crackpots make a living by reading cards or tea leaves and glaring into crystal balls at county fairs. *It's a joke! Unreal! You can't believe stuff like that.* Yet, Sky doesn't appear to be anything like that, and she's dead serious.

I know I have to really think this through. *Maybe I shouldn't see her anymore. How do I tell her that? How do I convince myself of that? Who can I talk to about this? The guys-Hell, no! God! Wouldn't the guys love this...I can hear them now...Sig, get your girlfriend to tell my fortune... what's my love life look like, sweetie?* That makes my blood boil and my gut clench. *What's wrong with me? I can deal with this. I can. No, I can't. I've just punched two gaping holes in my laundry bag...*

I don't call her or see her again this week. I spend my time looking up articles on clairvoyance and psychic abilities. It turns out there are legitimate psychics. Most genuine psychics don't work the county fair. Some work for police departments helping to solve crimes. *So my impression of psychics is a little skewed. That's a relief.*

I text her: Been busy at work. Concert at Interlochen on Sunday? Concert's at seven. Early dinner before? Pick you up around five? Sorry if it seems like I've overreacted. Sky texts back within a couple of minutes: YES!

Chapter 18

SKY

I'm well aware of my abilities as a clairvoyant. I also know I'm extremely accurate. *That's the way it is with the women in my family, we Arrowsons. We're an entire family of clairvoyants, at least the women are.* The *sight,* as we call it, doesn't flow strongly in the males, just in the females.

Tonight, I'm having a more futuristic vision, kinda weird and vague. By that I mean that I'm having difficulty pinning down just exactly when it might actually occur. Usually, I get visual clues that help pinpoint a time frame for a vision. I can tell if it's past by the way the people are dressed, what they are doing, etc. Yet, when everything looks close to the present, it gets harder to tell and that could mean the future, but I haven't had too many future visions.

This vision involves my friend and co-worker, Mia, and the guy she's been dating, Cory. They seem so happy together. So, when the vision starts, I'm excited:

A lot of women wear expensive jewelry. One woman's ruby necklace sparkles in candlelight. A robed priest waits at the altar of a church. Stained glass windows line the walls of the sanctuary. Every pew is filled to capacity. Cory wears a white tux and is standing next to the priest along with three groomsmen. They are watching the bride coming down the aisle. Organ music plays in the background. Cory breaks into a smile as he stares into the veiled face of his bride....

How exciting! Mia and Cory getting married! Mia's birthday is just days away, and she might be getting engaged. She did mention that she secretly hopes he will ask her to marry him on her birthday. This could be fun!

When I arrive at work, Mia is already there. Grabbing my coffee mug, I head for the nurse's station. This is where I find Mia, logging onto the hospital's intranet system. "So, Mia, have you picked up the latest issue of Brides?"

She's amused; her brown eyes sparkle at me. "Not yet. Why?"

"Just curious is all."

She smiles. "You've seen something haven't you?"

"Maybe." Mia is aware of my gifts. A smile tugs at the corners of my mouth.

She squeals. "What did you see? Will he ask me tomorrow?"

"I can't really say, but things seem positive."

Mia is ecstatic. "We're supposed to have dinner tomorrow night. I can't wait!" The spark lit, we whisper back and forth all night long about weddings.

"...I always dreamed of my bridesmaids wearing multicolored chiffon dresses with full skirts that flutter and float as they walk," Mia bubbles.

"What colors?" I query.

"Oh, I want a spring wedding, so blues and greens, pinks and yellows...."

"Spring?"

"Yes! Gotta be April or May," Mia gushes.

After my shift ends, I head for my early morning Zumba class, which lasts about an hour. By nine o'clock in the morning, I'm home in bed. As I start to nod off, I have the vision, for a second time:

> *I see Cory with the bride…they stand together at the altar…That's when I notice things aren't quite right: The fabric on the bridesmaids' gowns is too heavy for a spring wedding-velvety. And the colors are wrong-various shades of red. My attention is drawn to the bride who is wearing a long sleeved gown with a deep dip in the back that exposes her fair skin. Fair skin...hum...that's odd. Mia's complexion is darker than that.*

My next shift with Mia is three days after her birthday. She is less than enthusiastic and avoids talking to me. I finally corner her and learn that Cory sent Mia a dozen pink roses and took her out for a nice dinner, and they went dancing on her birthday. That was all. A sad and hurt look fills Mia's eyes every time I see her after that, and a stilted tone creeps into our conversations. It's hard to tell which one of us feels worse, Mia or me. Several weeks go by and still no proposal. In fact, Mia says she is seeing less and less of Cory.

In quiet moments, I try to concentrate on Cory, hoping to prompt a vision. Yet, I know what is true for my mother and aunt, is also true for me - *we see what we see when we see it.* We can't control what we see or when we see it. And we can't hear anything in visions. The frustration nearly drives me to distraction.

Three weeks later, Mia and Cory have all but broken up. She tells me that whenever the discussion broaches their relationship, Cory always changes the subject. Following this, I have the third and final vision while showering, as warm sudsy water washes over me:

Cory and the bride stand at the altar…he lifts her veil…they kiss, then turn and walk back up the aisle together, smiling…Cory with his pretty fair skinned, blonde haired bride.

I'm suddenly feeling like I've been punched in the stomach; the wind knocked out of me. *Cory isn't marrying Mia. He's marrying someone else. Oh my God! What have I done? My vision wasn't complete. I spoke too soon. I added to Mia's disappointment, hurting my friend.* This upsets me terribly. *Does Mia even know about the other woman? Is Cory cheating on her?*

That night, my distress is obvious to Sig. The moment he sees me he asks, "What's wrong? You look like you're going to cry."

"I feel like crying. I really do. I've hurt my friend, Mia, and I didn't mean to!"

"What happened?" Sig asks in a soothing voice.

"Just before her birthday, I hinted to Mia about a vision I had of her boyfriend, Cory. Mia and Cory have been dating for about two years. Mia hoped he might give her an engagement ring for her birthday. I had a vision of Cory getting married, but not a complete one. Anyhow, Cory didn't ask her to marry him. Later I had another vision of Cory, but this time it was more complete. Cory is marrying someone else. I don't even think Mia knows about the other woman. What's worse, Cory may be cheating on her."

"Ouch!" Sig winces. "That sucks!" He hugs me. "Well, you probably shouldn't have said anything. Psychics aren't very accurate, I hear." I pull away and glower at him.

A week later, at his urging, we take Mia to Flames for the cocktail hour, and I try to explain to her what happened, what went wrong.

"Mia, I'm so sorry. I know what I saw, but sometimes visions aren't complete. They don't show everything. I shouldn't have said anything. I'm truly sorry! I didn't mean to hurt you."

"It's ok. You didn't." Tears roll down her cheeks. "What really hurt was a friend of ours saw Cory at the movies with another woman after he told me he was going to a guy friend's house to 'game'. And I believed him!"

"Mia!" Handing her a tissue, I lean over and give her a hug. Feelings of guilt claw me with the fury of a giant lobster.

My lapse in judgment becomes Sig's primary justification for dismissing my abilities as a clairvoyant altogether. I, however, note one very important fact about this experience-I have had a vision of the distant future, something I have never experienced before. I can see more than just a few hours or days ahead. I clearly am able to see both the past and future, something neither my mother, nor my aunt, can do.

In spite of the discord my abilities have caused in our relationship, Sig and I are still seeing each other. In fact, we're spending three nights a week or more together. It's now late December, almost Christmas. That energy flowing between us is as strong as ever. We've been together for four months, but we've never been more physically intimate than kissing. *His self-control's amazing! I'm not sure why though. I thought I'd given positive signals, and I've even given him plenty of opportunities. My uniformed lion hasn't taken the bait. Why?*

Tonight, he's taking me to a party with friends from his base, his 'family'. He talks about them all the time. It'll be the first time I've actually met them. I'm nervous. My palms sweat, and I shiver a little now and then.

Carefully, I apply my makeup and select my clothes, choosing a pair of dark brown wool pants, an ivory silk tee, and a suede vest. I braid my hair and then add a peach scarf for a pop of color. Pearl studs and necklace add sparkle. Brown snow boots and a parka are necessary, since we have eight inches of snow on the ground with the weathermen predicting another six by morning. I can't eat; my stomach's too queasy. Instead, I sip hot tea and choke down a few crackers.

When he arrives at my door, he's wearing gold corduroys and a flannel shirt with a brown tweed jacket. Those colors, along with the waves in his rusty hair, excite me. After a few minutes, Sig says, "I didn't think you'd want to ride my bike to the party tonight, so I borrowed Mark's car. Kylee and Mark are taking hers."

"Right, the bike wouldn't work too well on a night like this. Thanks."

"I know this can get awkward, at first. They're good people. I know you'll fit right in."

I smile at him, even though my insides are shaking. "I'm sure it'll be fine."

And it was fine. His friends and coworkers seemed to be happy to meet me and fill me in on Sig's flirtatious habits before I entered his life. He blushes several times, but takes it with good humor. We never mention my Eri bloodline or my healer status. It doesn't come up. I am simply the nurse midwife, who delivered Tracy Rose, and that's how we met.

On the way home, Sig gives a deep sigh. "I've been a little nervous about how this was going to go," he admits.

"Why?"

"Because of all the stuff they told you about my being a flirt. You know...I didn't know how you'd take it. I didn't know if you'd be embarrassed to be seen with me or just mad and not want to see me ever again."

"And here I was worried about whether they'd accept a healer or not."

We're still laughing when he pulls up to my apartment complex. "Come in," I say. Once inside, I head for the kitchen to get some beers. Sig blocks my way. "Sky, I want something more tonight than another beer, I mean."

"Oh?"

"I want you."

"What took you so long?" I whisper.

"It's a sign of respect among my people."

I giggle; he tries to stop that by kissing me. I don't remember anything that happened between that moment and the bedroom, and I really don't care. I bed my lion.

Chapter 19
SIG

It's January when I finally meet Sky's family, her entire family. I like her parents, Katie and Sam Arrowson, her Aunt Faye, and Uncle Aden too. They're really nice folks, warm and welcoming. I'm pleasantly surprised to learn Aden is with the county police. Her dad owns a business, Sam the Handyman, right in the center of town. Her brothers, Micah and Carl, work for their dad.

Carl's an army vet. He's got a wife, Sarah, and a daughter, Rae. The kid's really cute and sharp as a whip. I can't figure what to make of Micah, Sky's oldest brother. He seems pretty quiet and reserved. I steer clear of him. But Faye and Aden Strongbow's twin sons, Paul, and Silas, are closer to my age and pretty ok guys. They seem to like me. Silas is a U.S. Park Ranger and Paul's Coast Guard, like me. He's stationed over at Sault Ste. Marie. I spend a lot of time talking with the 'dynamic duo' as the family calls them.

I don't want to offend anyone, but after a while, I extricate myself from the twins' conversation and try to locate Sky. From what I can tell, this is a close family. They seem to have lots to say to each other, exchanging news with a little local gossip thrown in for good measure. The only sign of tension I pick up on is between Katie and Sarah. *Not gonna even go there.*

Finding Sky with Micah watching a movie, I plop down on the floor in front of her. The movie is only mildly interesting, one of the Star Treks. I've seen it a dozen times. I use this time to survey my surroundings.

The Arrowson's cabin is right on Torch Lake. It's a spacious enough house, four bedrooms, a loft, and a huge stone fireplace. The kitchen is to the right side as you enter the front door and faces into the great room. Opposite the kitchen is the fireplace. The sitting area is arranged around the fireplace. Bedrooms are off to the left, and there's a dining nook where the table is piled high with food.

I was wowed by the fireplace when I first entered the house. Sky said, "Mom actually cooks meals in this fireplace sometimes." The Arrowsons and Strongbows are good cooks. I finally managed to roll away from the table without an empty spot left in my overstretched stomach.

Although we haven't talked about it too much, this clairvoyance stuff does make for some tense moments between us. On the way home, Sky describes some of her visions to me. One that catches my attention right away is when she sees the beginnings of some ancient battle taking place as an army storms a fortress. Almost all the people in the fortress die. Sky says her family members all see these same visions, which she calls 'shared.' She claims they can even see these visions together by "communing," linking their minds through some sort of focused concentration or meditation. I just listen.

I don't doubt she believes she has psychic abilities, "gifts" as she calls them. I know it would mean a lot to her if I said I supported her in this. But I just don't buy it. From what I've read, psychics don't have a very high accuracy rating. Besides, she even admits she doesn't have full control over this stuff. I know she really wants my approval, but personally, I'm just not ready to invest too much faith in it. I'm practical. Also, I keep remembering the Mia and Cory mess. For now, holding my tongue seems to be the best thing to do.

Chapter 20

SKY

It appears Sig and I have reached a nonverbal agreement not to discuss my gifts. I understand that there's no way he's ever going to fully accept this aspect of my life. Any further discussion seems pointless. Sig's the kinda guy who makes up his mind about something and that's the way it is, period. End of discussion. This hurts me deeply. Still, neither one of us is ready to give up. Not yet, anyway. We're still exploring the depth of feelings we have for each other. I know we'll have to have it out at some point, and I dread the day.

On the other hand, the rest of our relationship is good. We've become inseparable. I've introduced him to my friends and family; I've met his friends. Soon, I'll get to meet his real family. We're going to his sister's graduation. We've already gotten approval for the time off. Yesterday, we bought the tickets. We'll be flying to Baltimore, for a four day weekend, come May. He's already told his family about me too. It's now late April, so we only have about five weeks before we leave. I can't remember ever being more excited, nervous, and happy, all at the same time.

My terror begins just after we arrive home from the graduation. As I finish a ten hour delivery, and while my patient, along with her newborn, is wheeled from the room on a gurney, I see:

Sig and Dave in a copter. It hovers in midair, holding its position. I see the missile approach then, suddenly, the explosion.

In the birthing room, I grab for the door jam and sink slowly down the wall to the floor. It's so real, so intense I can almost smell the fumes. Shock floods through my veins like a dam burst. Horror registers on my face. My heart crumbles into tiny pieces, shattering inside me. My vision blurs, and sounds become indecipherable. Mia tries to catch me as I go down. Kneeling on the floor beside me, giving me a gentle shake, she says, "Sky! What's wrong? What's wrong?" My breathing becomes irregular. I can't respond. I can't even think. I stare blankly into her eyes, until everything goes dark.

I have the same vision several more times over the next few weeks. It takes me a while to be able to tell Sig. When I finally do, he listens but shakes his head in disbelief. He tries to quiet my panic, reassuring me of how much he loves me. He says, "Nothing's going to happen." Several very heated discussions about my gifts progress into full out fights. He refuses to believe what I'm telling him. Every fight ends with love making, so intense I feel our souls touch. I plead with him to take me seriously, but he shrugs it off.

August sees trees dressed in deep shades of green. Pine, oak, and ash branches sporadically cast slender shadows that dip and sway with the subtlest of breezes. Overhead, clear blue skies are filled with white fluffy clouds floating on currents of sunshine. And everywhere, heat beats down on the earth with the intensity of a furnace.

Above me a ceiling fan buzzes. A noisy lawnmower whirrs in the distance while snickering and raillery barge through my open sliding glass doors like bad breath. Chatter emanates from two guys working on their motorcycles in the parking lot below my balcony.

My second floor apartment is bathed in heat like a sauna. Sunlight leaves only a few jagged corners of the room and patches of floor space drenched in shadow. On the glass coffee table, my cellphone rings.

I grab for it, "Skylar Arrowson."

Sig's voice washes over me like a cool breeze. "Sky, I'm on my way over."

"Ok."

"I've got some good news and some bad news."

"Do I get a hint?" I query.

"I'll tell you when I get there. Love you, bye."

"Love you." I head for the shower. It's Sunday, the first day of my weekend, and I plan to spend it wrapped in Sig's arms.

A half hour later, as I open the door, I know I look good. My hair is swept to the side, flowing down my right shoulder. My white lacy tee and jean cutoffs set off my bare skin, and my face is natural, no makeup. Sig eyes me with approval as he steps through the doorway. His eyes glow at me, as I move away from the door leading him into the room.

"So, what's this news?" I give him a quizzical look as I head for the kitchen. The galley kitchen is to the left just inside the door with a black countertop. Three black stools line the bar. Sig passes the kitchen, making the corner into the dining room, "You want the good news first or the bad?" He grins, landing on one of the stools, opposite me.

"The bad news. Will it be beer or wine?"

"Wine, please."

I open a cupboard and withdraw two wine glasses, reaching into a drawer for the cork screw. At the same time, Sig pulls a bottle of merlot off the wine rack in the dining room. After he opens the bottle, I pour. Picking up his glass he tells me, "I'm going to be making supply drops, maybe some rescue missions. I'll be gone for at least a month, probably more."

I'm stunned; standing rigid, my body frozen. The love of my life is about to fulfill the vision that has been terrorizing my every waking moment. It's become my worst nightmare. I take a deep breath and exhale slowly. "When?" I pick up my wine and gently swirl it, watching the deep red color painting the insides of the glass.

"Day after tomorrow."

"Sig, please don't go!" I can't keep the hysteria out of my voice; it quivers. I drop my glass. He catches it. We grab paper towels and clean up the mess.

"Sky, I have my orders! We've been over this."

"Yes, but my vision...I've told you what I've seen. I'm a legitimate clairvoyant Sig! I know what I'm talking about!"

"You haven't had any formal training, and you're not always accurate. Remember Mia and Cory?"

"I was accurate! My vision was just incomplete!"

"Maybe this one isn't complete either, Sky." He soothes.

"Don't do this, please dear God! Don't do this! I can't handle it if...!"

"Nothing's going to happen. I fly missions all the time. I'm careful. You know it. I'm good at what I do." Silence, then he clears his throat, "Now for the good news...."

"What could possibly be good news?" *Why won't you believe me? Dear God, don't let him go this time. Please! Please make him listen!* He pulls something out of his pocket and sets it on the bar in front of me. I see a small velvet jewelry box. He opens it and shows me the sparkling round diamond ring with bright gold band.

"Oh!" I gasp.

"Do you like it? It was my grandmother's diamond. I had it reset. I hope it fits." He slides the ring onto my finger. "Marry me?" I'm too stunned for words. "Sky, will you marry me?"

"YEAH!"

We spend my weekend together, making love– two desperate souls pushing back barriers of time. He making plans for our wedding; I clinging to him, even as I feel him slipping away. When we part, he promises to call me. "I'll call every day."

The moment he leaves, the agony begins. I can't stand up without holding onto something. *Please God don't let it happen. I promise I'll do anything to have Sig alive and here with me again.*

Sig keeps his word. He calls me every afternoon around four, until the third week, on a Tuesday–the same day my home pregnancy test reads positive.

Officially, there was a mechanical malfunction of one of the missile launches on a nearby naval carrier. Sig was blown out of the sky in a case of "friendly fire."

Chapter 21

Columbia, MD 2016

SEVAN

It's a couple of weeks after Mark's birth, early April, and the end of a long hard day. Everyone has already gone home. As I'm locking up the shop, an Orthodox priest suddenly appears. Opening the door to speak with him, he explains he is here to deliver, personally, an eagle head cane, a small vial of oil, and a note from the Confessor.

The priest says, "He wanted you to have these. I promised to deliver them as soon as he had passed. I came immediately."

Incredulously, I ask, "He's dead? The Confessor is dead?"

"He passed about an hour ago, peacefully, in his sleep." The news lights up the dark space inside me with the force of a bomb. I tremble. My legs feel weak. I'd always sensed a mysterious connection with The Confessor and now I could feel it too. Thanking the priest, I accept the gifts and lock the door.

Opening the note, I read:

Sevan,

I bestow upon you this cane, a symbol of your duty as an Instrument of Justice, along with the vial. May the cane support you as it has those who came before you. May it ease your burden as it has mine, a burden I lay down and you now take up. The vial is a legacy of the Light; its content is mercy and healing. Use it wisely.

Know that the Light loves both justice and mercy. For those who walk in it or follow it, their mission is unique to them.

My earthly mission is complete; my life's work now done. Those of us who have walked in grave darkness are born again in Light. Believe!

I have already anointed you, thereby passing my torch. Remember, your purpose is one which only the Light ordains.

Now and Forever,
Shalom

Made in the USA
Middletown, DE
01 November 2023